'His child's voice is immensely powerful and is an extraordinary testament to the human desire for survival. Not only did Dave Pelzer survive, he triumphed . . . Essentially, The Lost Boy is a story of regeneration and resilience, as well as harrowing pain . . . What has made Dave Pelzer's story a bestseller is that it is also a story of redemption. It is a story where love, kindness, patience and endurance triumph'

*Daily Mail*

'The tale of how he survived the really bad abuse of his early life makes for inspirational, if incredibly sad, reading'

*Manchester Evening News*

'It takes a personal testimony like Dave Pelzer's to bring home the horrors of child abuse – the secrecy, the shame, the struggle to survive' Bel Mooney, *Mail on Sunday*

'The three books tell a harrowing tale with vast dignity – and not a trace of psychobabble' *Independent*

'Pelzer is able to continue his dreadful story in an admirably dispassionate style. He lets you see what was going on through the eyes of the child he once was but, because he has doggedly taught himself not to hate, his voice is never shrill or hysterical. It is this cool tone that makes what he has to say even more compelling' Penny Perrick, *The Times*

'The raw simplicity of this honest account keeps the pages turning as the reader stays abreast with David's recovery. If ever a book demonstrated the power of the human spirit to triumph in adversity, this is it. An inspirational book which teaches resilience and forgiveness' *Birmingham Post*

'This heartfelt true story of one child's courage to survive cannot fail to move you' *Heat*

# A
# Child
# Called 'It'

Dave Pelzer

An Orion paperback

First published in Great Britain in 2000
by Orion Media
This paperback edition published in 2012
by Orion Books Ltd,
Orion House, 5 Upper St Martin's Lane,
London WC2H 9EA

An Hachette UK company

1 3 5 7 9 10 8 6 4 2

A CIP catalogue record for this book
is available from the British Library.

ISBN 978-1-4091-3844-0

Typeset by Deltatype Ltd, Birkenhead, Merseyside

Printed and bound in Great Britain by
Clays Ltd, St Ives plc

The Orion Publishing Group's policy is to use papers that
are natural, renewable and recyclable products and
made from wood grown in sustainable forests. The logging
and manufacturing processes are expected to conform to
the environmental regulations of the country of origin.

www.orionbooks.co.uk

This book is dedicated to my son Stephen, who, by the grace of God, has taught me the gift of love and joy through the eyes of a child.

This book is also dedicated to the teachers and staff members of Thomas Edison Elementary School to include:

Steven E. Ziegler
Athena Konstan
Peter Hansen
Joyce Woodworth
Janice Woods
Betty Howell
and the School Nurse

To all of you, for your courage and for putting your careers on the line that fateful day, 5 March 1973. You saved my life.

# Contents

# *Acknowledgments*

After years of intensive labor, sacrifice, frustration, compromises and deception, this book is finally **published** and available in bookstores everywhere. I wish to take a moment and pay homage to those who truly believed in this crusade.

To Jack Canfield, co-author of the phenomenal bestseller *Chicken Soup for the Soul,* for his extreme kindness and opening a big door. Jack is indeed a rare entity who, without reservation, assists more individuals in a single day than many of us can help in a lifetime. Bless you, sir.

To Nancy Mitchell and Kim Wiele at the Canfield Group for their enormous enthusiasm and guidance. Thank you, ladies.

To Peter Vegso at Health Communications, Inc., as well as Christine Belleris, Matthew Diener, Kim Weiss and the entire friendly staff at HCI for their honesty, professionalism and everyday courtesy that make publishing a pleasure. Kudos galore to Irene Xanthos and Lori Golden for their tenacious drive and for picking up the slack. And a gargantuan thank you to the Art Department for all your hard work and dedication.

A special thank you to Marsha Donohoe, editor extraordinaire, for her hours of re-editing and eradicating 'the Wahoo' out of the tome (that's 'book' for those of you who reside in Yuba/Sutter Counties in Northern CA), so to provide the reader with a clear, precise sense of this story through the eyes of a child. For Marsha, it was a matter of '. . . Farmer's Trust.'

To Patti Breitman, of Breitman Publishing Projects, for her initial work and for giving it a good run for the money.

To Cindy Adams for her unwavering faith when I needed it the most.

A special thank you to Ric & Don at the Rio Villa Resort, my then home away from home, for providing the perfect sanctuary during the process of this project.

And lastly, to Phyllis Colleen. I wish you happiness. I wish you peace. May God bless you.

# Author's Notes

Some of the names in this book have been changed in order to maintain the dignity and privacy of others.

This book, the first part of the trilogy, depicts language that was developed from a child's viewpoint. The tone and vocabulary reflect the age and wisdom of the child at that particular time.

This book is based on the child's life from ages 4 to 12. The second part of the trilogy, *The Lost Boy*, is based on his life from ages 12 to 18. The final part of the trilogy, *A Man Named Dave*, is based on his adult life.

Chapter 1

# The Rescue

5 March 1973, Daly City, California – *I'm late. I've got to finish the dishes on time, otherwise no breakfast; and since I didn't have dinner last night, I have to make sure I get something to eat. Mother's running around yelling at my brothers. I can hear her stomping down the hallway towards the kitchen. I dip my hands back into the scalding rinse water. It's too late. She catches me with my hands out of the water.*

*SMACK! Mother hits me in the face, and I topple to the floor. I know better than to stand there and take the hit. I learned the hard way that she takes that as an act of defiance, which means more hits, or worst of all, no food. I regain my posture and dodge her looks, as she screams into my ears.*

*I act timid, nodding to her threats. 'Please,' I say to myself, 'just let me eat. Hit me again, but I have to* have food.' *Another blow pushed my head against the tile counter top. I let the tears of mock defeat stream down my face as she storms out of the kitchen, seemingly satisfied with herself. After I count her steps, making sure she's gone, I breathe a sigh of relief. The act worked. Mother can beat me all she wants, but I haven't let her take away my will to somehow survive.*

*I finish the dishes, then my other chores. For my reward I receive breakfast – leftovers from one of my brothers' cereal bowls. Today it's Lucky Charms. There are only a few bits of cereal left in a half of a bowl of milk, but as quickly as I can, I swallow it before Mother changes her mind. She has done that before, Mother enjoys using food as her weapon. She knows better than to throw leftovers in the garbage can. She knows I'll dig it out later. Mother knows most of my tricks.*

*Minutes later I'm in the old family station wagon. Because I'm so late with my chores, I have to be driven to school. Usually I run to school, arriving just as class begins, with no time to steal any food from other kids' lunch boxes.*

*Mother drops my oldest brother off, but keeps me for a lecture about her plans for me tomorrow. She is going to take me to her brother's house. She says Uncle Dan will* 'take care of me.' She makes it a threat. I give her a frightened look as if I am truly afraid. But I know that even though my uncle is a hard-nosed man, he surely won't treat me like Mother does.

Before the station wagon comes to a complete stop, I dash out of the car. Mother yells for me to return. I have forgotten my crumpled lunch bag, which has always had the same menu for the last three years – two peanut butter sandwiches and a few carrot sticks. Before I bolt out of the car again, she says, 'Tell 'em ... Tell 'em you ran into the door.' Then in a voice she rarely uses with me, she states, 'Have a nice day.' I look into her swollen red eyes. She still has a hangover from last night's stupor. Her once beautiful, shiny black hair is now frazzled clumps. As usual, she wears no makeup. She is overweight, and she knows it. In all, this has become Mother's typical look.

Because I am so late, I have to report to the administrative office. The gray-haired secretary greets me with a smile. Moments later, the school nurse comes out and leads me into her office, where we go through the normal routine. First, she examines my face and arms. 'What's that above your eye?' she asks.

---

*I nod sheepishly, 'Oh, I ran into the hall door . . . by accident.'*

*Again she smiles and takes a clipboard from the top of a cabinet. She flips through a page or two, then bends down to show me. 'Here,' she points to the paper, 'you said that last Monday. Remember?'*

*I quickly change my story, 'I was playing baseball and got hit by the bat. It was an accident.' Accident. I am always supposed to say that. But the nurse knows better. She scolds me so I'll tell the truth. I always break down in the end and confess, even though I feel I should protect my mother.*

*The nurse tells me that I'll be fine and asks me to take off my clothes. We have been doing this since last year, so I immediately obey. My long-sleeve shirt has more holes than Swiss cheese. It's the same shirt I've worn for about two years. Mother has me wear it every day as her way to humiliate me. My pants are just as bad, and my shoes have holes in the toes. I can wiggle my big toe out of one of them. While I stand clothed only in my underwear, the nurse records my various marks and bruises on the clipboard. She counts the slash-like marks on my face, looking for any she might have missed in the past. She is very thorough. Next, the nurse opens my mouth to look at my teeth that are chipped from having been slammed against the kitchen tile counter top. She jots a few more notes on the paper. As she continues to look me over, she stops at the old scar on my stomach. 'And that,' she says as she takes a deep swallow, 'is where she stabbed you?'*

*'Yes, ma'am,' I reply. 'Oh no!' I tell myself, 'I've done something wrong . . . again.' The nurse must have seen the concern in my eyes. She puts the clipboard down and hugs me. 'God,' I tell myself, 'She is so warm.' I don't want to let go. I want to stay in her arms forever. I hold my eyes tightly shut, and for a few moments nothing else exists. She pats my head. I flinch from the swollen bruise Mother gave me this morning. The nurse then breaks the embrace and leaves the room. I rush to put my clothes back on. She doesn't know it, but I do everything as fast as possible.*

*The nurse returns in a few minutes with Mr Hansen the principal, and two of my teachers, Miss Woods and Mr Ziegler. Mr Hansen knows me very well. I've been in his office more than any other kid in school. He looks at the paper, as the nurse reports her findings. He lifts my chin. I'm afraid to look into his eyes, which is mostly a habit from trying to deal with my mother. But it's also because I don't want to tell him anything. Once, about a year ago, he called Mother to ask about my bruises. At that time, he had no idea what was really going on. He just knew I was a troubled kid who was stealing food. When I came to school the next day, he saw the results of Mother's beatings. He never called her again.*

*Mr Hansen barks he's had enough of this. I almost leap out of my skin with fear. 'He's going to call Mother again!' my brain screams. I break down and cry. My body shakes like jello and I mumble like a baby, begging Mr Hansen not to phone Mother. 'Please!' I whine, 'Not today! Don't you understand, it's Friday?'*

*Mr Hansen assures me he's not going to call Mother, and sends me off to class. Since it's too late for homeroom class, I sprint directly to Mrs Woodworth's English class. Today's a spelling test on all the states and their capitals. I'm not prepared. Usually I'm a very good student, but for the past few months I gave up on everything in my life, including escaping my misery through my schoolwork.*

*Upon entering the room, all the students plug their noses and hiss at me. The substitute teacher, a younger woman, waves her hands in front of her face. She's not used to my smell. At arms length she hands my test to me, but before I can take my seat in the back of the class by an open window, I'm summoned back to the principal's office. The entire room lets out a howl at me – the reject of the fifth grade.*

*I run to the administration office, and I'm there in a flash. My throat is raw and still burns from yesterday's 'game' Mother played against me. The secretary leads me into the teachers' lounge. After she opens the door, it takes a moment for my eyes to adjust. In front of me, sitting around a table, are my homeroom teacher Mr Ziegler, my math teacher Miss Woods, the school nurse, Mr Hansen and a police officer. My feet become frozen. I don't know whether to run away or wait for the roof to cave in. Mr Hansen waves me in, as the secretary closes the door behind me. I take a seat at the head of the table, explaining I didn't steal anything ... today. Smiles break everyone's depressed frowns. I have no idea that they are about to risk their jobs to save me.*

*The police officer explains why Mr Hansen called him. I can feel myself shrink into the chair. The officer asks that I tell him about Mother. I shake my head no. Too many people already know the secret, and I know she'll find out. A soft voice calms me. I think it's Miss Woods. She tells me it's all right. I take a deep breath, wring my hands and reluctantly tell them about Mother and I.*

*Then the nurse has me stand up and show the policeman the scar on my chest. Without hesitation, I tell them it was an accident; which it was – Mother never meant to stab me. I cry as I spill my guts, telling them Mother punishes me because I am bad. I wish they would leave me alone. I feel so slimy inside. I know after all these years there is nothing anyone can do.*

*A few minutes later, I am excused to sit in the outer office. As I close the door, all the adults look at me and shake their heads in an approving way. I fidget in my chair, watching the secretary type papers. It seems forever before Mr Hansen calls me back into the room. Miss Woods and Mr Ziegler leave the lounge. They seem happy, but at the same time worried. Miss Woods kneels down and wraps me in her arms. I don't think I will ever forget the smell of the perfume in her hair. She lets go, turning away so I won't see her cry. Now I am really worried. Mr Hansen gives me a lunch tray from the cafeteria. 'My God! Is it lunch time already?' I ask myself.*

*I gobble down the food so fast I can hardly taste it. I finish the tray in record time. Soon the principal returns with a box of cookies, warning me not to eat so fast. I have no idea what's going on. One of my guesses is that my father, who is separated from my mother, has come to get me. But I know it's a fantasy. The policeman asks for my address and telephone number.* 'That's it!' *I tell myself.* 'It's back to hell! I'm going to get it from her again!'

*The officer writes down more notes as Mr Hansen and the school nurse look on. Soon he closes his note pad and tells Mr Hansen that he has enough information. I look up at the principal. His face is covered with sweat. I can feel my stomach start to coil. I want to go to the bathroom and throw up.*

*Mr Hansen opens the door, and I can see all the teachers on their lunch break staring at me. I'm so ashamed.* 'They know,' *I tell myself.* 'They know the truth about my mother; the real truth.' *It is so important for them to know that I'm not a bad boy. I want so much to be liked, to be loved. I turn down the hall. Mr Ziegler is holding Miss Woods. She is crying. I can hear her sniffle. She gives me another hug and quickly turns away. Mr Ziegler shakes my hand.* 'Be a good boy,' *he says.*

'Yes, sir. I'll try,' *is all I can say.*

*The school nurse stands in silence beside Mr Hansen. They all tell me goodbye. Now I know I am going to jail.*

---

'Good,' *I tell myself.* 'At least she won't be able to beat me if I'm in jail.'

*The police officer and I walk outside, past the cafeteria. I can see some of the kids from my class playing dodge ball. A few of them stop playing. They yell, 'David's busted! David's busted!' The policeman touches my shoulder, telling me everything is okay. As he drives me up the street, away from Thomas Edison Elementary School, I see some kids who seem to be fazed by my departure. Before I left, Mr Ziegler told me he would tell the other kids the truth – the real truth. I would give anything to have been there in class when they found out I'm not so bad.*

*In a few minutes, we arrive at the Daly City Police Station. I sort of expect Mother to be there. I don't want to get out of the car. The officer opens the door and gently takes me by the elbow, into a big office. No other person is in the room. The policeman sits in a chair, in the corner, where he types several sheets of paper. I watch the officer closely as I slowly eat my cookies. I savor them as long as I can. I don't know when I will be eating again.*

*It's past 1:00 P.M. when the policeman finishes his paperwork. He asks for my telephone number again.*

'Why?' I whine.

'I have to call her, David,' he says gently.

'No!' I command. 'Send me back to school. Don't you get it? She mustn't find out I told!'

He calms me down with another cookie, as he slowly dials 7-5-6-2-4-6-0. I watch the black dial turn as I get up and walk towards him, straining my whole body while trying to hear the phone ringing on the other end. Mother answers. Her voice scares me. The policeman waves me away, and takes a deep breath before saying, 'Mrs Pelzer, this is Officer Smith from the Daly City Police Department. Your son David will not be coming home today. He will be in the custody of the San Matao Juvenile Department. If you have any questions, you can call them.' He hangs up the phone and smiles. 'Now that wasn't so hard, was it?' he asks me. But the look on his face tells me he is assuring himself, more than he is me.

A few miles later, we are on highway 280, heading towards the outskirts of Daly City. I look to my right and see a sign that reads, 'THE MOST BEAUTIFUL HIGHWAY IN THE WORLD.' The officer smiles with relief, as we leave the city limits. 'David Pelzer,' he says, 'you're free.'

'What?' I ask, clutching my only source of food. 'I

*don't understand. Aren't you taking me to some kind of jail?'*

*Again he smiles, and gently squeezes my shoulder. 'No, David. You have nothing to worry about, honest. Your mother is never going to hurt you again.'*

*I lean back against the seat. A reflection from the sun hits my eyes. I turn away from the rays as a single tear runs down my cheek.*

'I'm free?'

Chapter 2

# Good Times

In the years before I was abused, my family was the 'Brady Bunch' of the 1960s. My two brothers and I were blessed with the perfect parents. Our every whim was fulfilled with love and care.

We lived in a modest two-bedroom house, in what was considered a 'good' neighborhood in Daly City. I can remember looking out of our living room bay window on a clear day, to gaze at the bright orange towers of the Golden Gate Bridge and the beautiful skyline of San Francisco.

My father, Stephen Joseph, supported his family as a fireman, working in the heart of San Francisco. He stood about five feet ten inches tall, and he weighed about 190 pounds. He had broad shoulders and forearms that would make any muscle man proud. His thick black eyebrows matched his hair. I felt special when he winked at me and called me 'Tiger'.

My mother, Catherine Roerva, was a woman of average size and appearance. I never could remember the color of her hair or eyes, but Mom was a woman who glowed with love for her children. Her greatest asset was her determination. Mom always had ideas, and she always took command of all family matters. Once, when I was four or five years old, Mom said she was sick, and I remember feeling that she did not seem to be herself at all. It was a day when Father was working at the fire station. After serving dinner, Mom rushed from the table and began painting the steps that led to the garage. She coughed as she frantically brushed the red paint onto every step. The paint had not fully dried, when Mom began tacking rubber mats to the steps. The red paint was all over the mats and Mom. When she finished, Mom went into the house and collapsed on the couch. I remember asking her why she had put the mats down before the paint dried. She smiled and said, 'I just wanted to surprise your dad.'

When it came to housekeeping, Mom was an absolute clean fiend. After feeding my two brothers,

Ronald and Stan, and I breakfast, she would dust, disinfect, scour and vacuum everything. No room in our house was left untouched. As we grew older, Mom made sure we did our part by keeping our room neat. Outside, she meticulously attended a small flower garden, which was the envy of the neighborhood. With Mom, everything she touched turned into gold. She didn't believe in doing anything halfway. Mom often told us that we must always do the best we could, in whatever we did.

Mom was truly a gifted cook. Of all the things she did for her family, I think creating new and exotic meals was her favorite. This was especially true on those days when Father was home. Mom would spend the better part of the day preparing one of her fantastic meals. On some days when Father was working, Mom would take us on exciting sightseeing tours around the city. One day, she took us to Chinatown in San Francisco. As we drove around the area, Mom told us about the culture and history of the Chinese people. When we returned, Mom started her record player, and our home was filled with beautiful sounds from the Orient. She then decorated the dining room with Chinese lanterns. That evening, she dressed in a kimono and served what seemed to us a very exotic but delicious meal. At the end of dinner, Mom gave us fortune cookies and read the captions for us. I felt that the cookie's message would lead me to my destiny. Some years later, when I was old enough to read, I found one of my old fortunes. It said, 'Love and honor thy mother, for she is the fruit that gives thou life.'

Back then our house was full of pets – cats, dogs, aquariums filled with exotic fish and a gopher tortoise named 'Thor'. I remember the tortoise best because Mom let me pick a name for it. I felt proud because my brothers had been chosen to name the other pets and it was now my turn. I named the reptile after my favorite cartoon character.

The five- and ten-gallon aquariums seemed to be everywhere. There were at least two in the living room, and one filled with guppies in our bedroom. Mom creatively decorated the heated tanks with colored gravel and colored foil backs; anything she thought would make the tanks more realistic. We would often sit by the tanks while Mom told us about the different species of fish.

The most dramatic of Mom's lessons, came one

Sunday afternoon. One of our cats was behaving in an odd way. Mom had us all sit down by the cat while she explained the process of birth. After all the kittens had slipped safely out of the mother cat, Mom explained in great detail the wonder of life. No matter what the family was doing, she somehow came up with a constructive lesson; though we were not usually aware that we were being taught.

For our family – during those good years – the holidays started with Halloween. One October night, when the huge harvest moon was in full view, Mom hurried the three of us out of our house, to gaze at the 'Great Pumpkin' in the sky. When we returned to our bedroom, she told us to peek under our pillows where we found Matchbox race cars. My two brothers and I squealed with delight as Mom's face was flushed with pride.

The day after Thanksgiving, Mom would disappear to the basement, then bring up enormous boxes filled with Christmas decorations. While standing on a ladder, she tacked strings of ornaments to the ceiling beams. When she was finished, every room in our house had a seasonal touch. In the dining room Mom arranged different sizes of red candles on the counter of her prized oak hutch. Snowflake patterns graced every window in the living room and dining room. Christmas lights were draped around our bedroom windows. Every night I fell asleep while staring at the soft, colorful glow of the Christmas lights that blinked on and off.

Our Christmas tree was never ever an inch under eight feet, and it took the whole family hours to decorate it. Each year one of us was honored by being allowed to place the angel at the top of the tree, while Father held us up in his strong arms. After the tree was decorated and dinner was finished, we would pile into the station wagon and cruise the neighborhood, admiring the decorations on other homes. Mom always rambled on about her ideas of bigger and better things for the next Christmas, even though my brothers and I knew our house was always the best. When we returned home, Mom sat us down by the fireplace to drink egg nog. While she told us stories, Bing Crosby sang 'White Christmas' on the stereo. I was so excited during those holiday seasons that I couldn't sleep. Sometimes Mom would cradle me, while I fell asleep listening to the crackle of the fire.

As Christmas Day came nearer, my brothers and I

became more and more excited. The pile of gifts at the base of the tree grew day by day. By the time Christmas finally arrived, there were dozens of gifts for each of us.

On Christmas Eve, after a special dinner and caroling, we were allowed to open one gift. Afterwards, we were sent to bed. I always strained my ears as I laid in bed, waiting for the sound of Santa's sleigh bells. But I always fell asleep before I heard his reindeer land on the roof.

Before dawn, Mom would creep into our room and wake us, whispering, 'Santa came!' One year she gave each of us a yellow, plastic, Tonka hard hat and had us march into the living room. It took us forever to rip the colorful paper from the boxes, to discover our new Christmas toys. Afterwards, Mom had us run to the backyard in our new robes, to look back in through the window at our huge Christmas tree. That year, standing in the yard, I remember seeing Mom cry. I asked her why she was sad. Mom told me she was crying because she was so happy to have a real family.

Because Father's job often required him to work 24-hour shifts, Mother often took us on day trips to places like the nearby Golden Gate Park in San

Francisco. As we slowly drove through the park, Mom explained how the areas were different and how she envied the beautiful flowers. We always visited the park's Steinhart Aquarium last. My brothers and I would blaze up the stairs and charge through the heavy doors. We were thrilled as we leaned over the brass, sea-horse-shaped fence, looking far below at the small waterfall and pond that were home to the alligators and large turtles. As a child, this was my favorite place in the entire park. I once became frightened, as I thought about slipping through the barrier and falling into the pond. Without speaking a word, Mom must have felt my fear. She looked down at me and held my hand ever so softly.

Spring meant picnics. Mom would prepare a feast of fried chicken, salads, sandwiches and lots of deserts the night before. Early the next day, our family sped off to Junipero Serra Park. Once there, my brothers and I would run wild on the grass and pump higher and higher on the park's swings. Sometimes we would venture off on a new trail. Mom always had to pry us away from our fun, when it came time for lunch. We wolfed down our food, hardly tasting it, before my brothers and I blitzed off for parts unknown, in search of high adventure. Our parents seemed happy to lie next to each other on a blanket, sip red wine and watch us play.

It was always a thrill when the family went on summer vacation. Mom was always the mastermind behind these trips. She planned every detail, and swelled with pride as the activities came together. Usually we traveled to Portola or Memorial Park, and camped out in our giant, green tent for a week or so. But whenever Father drove us north across the Golden Gate Bridge, I knew we were going to my favorite place in the world – the Russian River.

The most memorable trip to the river for me, happened the year I was in kindergarten. On the last day of school, Mom asked that I be excused a half-hour early. As Father honked the horn, I rocketed up the small hill from the school, to the waiting car. I was excited because I knew where we were going. During the drive, I became fascinated at the seemingly endless fields of grapes. When we drove into the quiet town of Guerneville, I rolled my window down to smell the sweet air from the redwood trees.

Each day was a new adventure. My brothers and I either spent the day climbing an old, burnt tree stump with our special whomper-stomper boots or swimming in the river at Johnson's Beach. Johnson's Beach was a whole day's event. We would leave our cabin by nine and return after three. Mom taught each of us to swim in a small, trenched hole in the river. That summer Mom taught me how to swim on my back. She seemed so proud when I was finally able to do it.

Every day seemed sprinkled with magic. One day after dinner, Mom and Dad took the three of us to watch the sunset. All of us held hands, as we crept past Mr Parker's cabin to get to the river. The green river water was as smooth as glass. The bluejays scolded the other birds, and a warm breeze blew through my hair. Without a word, we stood watching the fireball-like sun as it sank behind the tall trees, leaving bright blue and orange streaks in the sky. From above, I felt someone hug my shoulders. I thought it was my father. I turned and became flushed with pride to find Mom holding me tightly. I could feel her heart beat. I never felt as safe and as warm as that moment in time, at the Russian River.

## Chapter 3
## Bad Boy

My relationship with Mom drastically changed from discipline that developed into a kind of lifestyle that grew out of control. It became so bad at times, I had no strength to crawl away – even if it meant saving my life.

As a small child, I probably had a voice that carried farther than others. I also had the unfortunate luck of getting caught at mischief, even though my brothers and I were often committing the same 'crime'. In the beginning, I was put in a corner of our bedroom. By this time, I had become afraid of Mom. Very afraid. I never asked her to let me come out. I would sit and wait for one of my brothers to come into our bedroom, and have him ask if David could come out now and play.

About this time, Mom's behavior began to change

radically. At times while Father was away at work, she would spend the entire day lying on the couch, dressed only in her bathrobe, watching television. Mom got up only to go to the bathroom, get another drink or heat leftover food. When she yelled at us, her voice changed from the nurturing mother to the wicked witch. Soon, the sound of Mother's voice began to send tremors down my spine. Even when she barked at one of my brothers, I'd run to hide in our room, hoping she would soon return to the couch, her drink and her TV show. After a while, I could determine what kind of day I was going to have by the way she dressed. I would breathe a sigh of relief whenever I saw Mom come out of her room in a nice dress with her face made up. On these days she always came out with a smile.

When Mother decided that the 'corner treatment' was no longer effective, I graduated to the 'mirror treatment'. In the beginning, it was a no-notice form of punishment. Mother would simply grab me and smash my face against the mirror, smearing my tear-streaked face on the slick, reflective glass. Then she would order me to say over and over again, 'I'm a bad boy! I'm a bad boy! I'm a bad boy!' I was then forced to stand, staring into the mirror. I would stand there with my hands locked to my sides, weaving back and forth, dreading the moment when the second set of television commercials aired. I knew Mother would soon be stomping down the hall to see if my face was still against the mirror, and to tell me what a sickening child I was. Whenever my brothers came into the room while I was at the mirror, they would look at me, shrug their shoulders and continue to play – as if I were not there. At first I was jealous, but soon I learned that they were only trying to save their own skins.

While Father was at work, Mother would often yell and scream while forcing my brothers and I to search the entire house for something she had lost. The quest usually started in the morning and lasted for hours. After a while, I was usually sent to search in the garage which was under part of the house – like a basement. Even there, I trembled upon hearing Mother scream at one of my brothers.

The searches continued for months, and finally, I was the only one singled out to look for her things. Once, I forgot what I was looking for. When I timidly asked her what it was that I was to find, Mother smacked me in the face. She was lying on the couch at the time, and she didn't even stop watching her television show. Blood gushed from my nose and I began to cry. Mother snatched a napkin from her table, tore a piece and rammed it up my nose. 'You know damn well what you're looking for!' she screamed. 'Now go find it!' I scurried back down to the basement, making sure I made enough noise to convince Mother I was feverishly obeying her command. As Mother's 'find the thing' became more common, I began to fantasize that I had found her missing item. I imagined myself marching upstairs with my prize and Mom greeting me with hugs and kisses. My fantasy included the family living happily ever after. But, I never found any of Mother's lost things, and she never let me forget that I was an incompetent loser.

As a small child, I realized Mom was as different as night and day when Father was home from work. When Mom fixed her hair and put on nice clothes, she seemed more relaxed. I loved it when Dad was home. It meant no beatings, mirror treatments or long searches for her missing things. Father became my protector. Whenever he went to the garage to work on a project, I followed him. If he sat in his favorite chair to read the newspaper, I parked myself at his feet. In the evenings, after the dinner dishes were cleared from the table, Father would wash them, and I would dry. I knew that as long as I stayed by his side, no harm would come to me.

One day before he left for work, I received a dreadful shock. After he said goodbye to Ron and Stan, he knelt down, held my shoulders tightly and told me to be a 'good boy'. Mother stood behind him with her arms folded across her chest, and a grim smile on her face. I looked into my father's eyes and knew right then that I was a 'bad boy'. An ice-cold chill rushed through my body. I wanted to hold on to him and never let go, but before I could give Father a hug, he stood up, turned and walked out the door, without saying another word.

For a short time after Father's warning, things seemed to calm down between Mother and I. When Dad was home, my brothers and I played in our room or outside, until about 3:00 P.M. Mother would then turn on the television so we could watch cartoons. For my parents, 3:00 P.M. meant 'Happy Hour'. Father would cover the kitchen counter top with bottles of alcohol and tall fancy glasses. He cut up lemons and limes, placing them in small bowls beside a small jar of cherries. They often drank from mid-afternoon, until my brothers and I climbed into bed. I remember watching them dance around the kitchen to music from the radio. They held each other close, and they looked so happy. I thought I could bury the bad times. I was wrong. The bad times were only beginning.

A month or two later, on a Sunday, while Father was at work, my brothers and I were playing in our room when we heard Mother rush down the hall, yelling at us. Ron and Stan ran for cover in the living room. I instantly sat down in my chair. With both arms stretched out and raised, Mother came at me. As she came closer and closer, I backed my chair towards the wall. Soon, my head touched the wall. Mother's eyes were glazed and red, and her breath smelled of booze. I closed my eyes as the oncoming blows began to rock me from side to side. I tried to protect my face with my hands, but Mother would only knock them away. Her punches seemed to last forever. Finally, I snaked my left arm up to cover my face. As Mother grabbed my arm, she lost her balance and staggered back a step. As she jerked violently to regain her stability, I heard something pop, and felt an intense pain in my shoulder and arm. The startled look on Mother's face told me that she had heard the sound too, but she released her grip on my arm, and turned and walked away as if nothing had happened. I cradled my arm as it began to throb with pain. Before I could actually inspect my arm, Mother summoned me to dinner.

I plopped down at a T.V. tray to try to eat. As I reached for a glass of milk, my left arm did not respond. My fingers twitched upon command, but my arm tingled and had become lifeless. I looked at Mother, trying to plead with my eyes. She ignored me. I knew something was very wrong, but I was too afraid to utter a word. I simply sat there, staring at my tray of food. Mother finally excused me and sent me to bed early, telling me to sleep in the top bunk. This was unusual because I had always slept on the bottom. Sometime near morning I finally fell asleep, with my left arm carefully cradled in the other.

I hadn't slept long when Mother awakened me, explaining that I had rolled out of the top bunk during the night. She seemed to be deeply concerned about my condition, as she drove me to the hospital. When she told the doctor about my fall from the top bunk bed, I could tell by the look he gave me that he knew my injury was no accident. Again, I was too afraid to speak up. At home, Mother made up an even more dramatic story for Father. In the new version, Mother included her efforts to catch me before I hit the floor. As I sat in Mother's lap, listening to her lie to Father, I knew my mom was sick. But my fear kept the accident our secret. I knew if I ever told anyone, the next 'accident' would be worse.

School was a haven for me. I was thrilled to be away from Mother. At recess I was a wild man. I blitzed through the bark-covered playground, looking for new, adventurous things to do. I made friends easily and felt so happy to be at school. One day in late spring, when I returned home from school, Mother threw me into her bedroom. She then yelled at me, stating I was to be held back from the first grade because I was a bad boy. I did not understand. I knew I had more 'happy face' papers than anybody in the class. I obeyed my teacher and I felt she liked me. But Mother continued to roar that I had shamed the family and would be severely punished. She decided that I was banned from watching television, forever. I was to go without dinner and accomplish whatever chores Mother could dream up. After another thrashing, I was sent to the garage to stand until Mother called me to go to bed.

That summer, without warning, I was dropped off at my Aunt Jose's house on the way to the campsite. No one told me about this and I could not understand why. I felt like an outcast as the station wagon drove away, leaving me behind. I felt so sad and hollow. I tried to run away from my aunt's house. I wanted to find my family, and for some strange reason, I wanted to be with Mother. I didn't get far, and my aunt later informed my mother of my attempt. The next time Father worked the 24-hour shift, I paid for my sin. Mother smacked, punched and kicked me until I crumpled to the floor. I tried to tell Mother that I had run away because I wanted to be with her and the family. I tried to tell her that I had missed her, but Mother refused to let me speak. I tried once more and Mother dashed to the bathroom, snatched a bar of soap and crammed it down my throat. After that, I was no longer allowed to speak unless I was instructed to do so.

Returning to the first grade was really a joy. I knew

the basic lessons and was instantly dubbed the class genius. Since I was held back, Stan and I were in the same grade. During recess, I would go over to Stan's first-grade class to play. At school we were the best of friends; however, at home, we both knew I was not to be acknowledged.

One day I rushed home to show off a school paper. Mother threw me into her bedroom, yelling about a letter she had received from the North Pole. She claimed the letter said that I was a 'bad boy' and Santa would not bring me any gifts for Christmas. Mother raged on and on, saying that I had embarrassed the family *again.* I stood in a daze, as Mother badgered me relentlessly. I felt I was living in a nightmare that Mother had created, and I prayed she would somehow wake up. Before Christmas that year, there were only a couple of gifts for me under the tree, and those came from relatives outside the immediate family. On Christmas morning, Stan dared to ask Mother why Santa had brought me only two paint-by-number pictures. She lectured him saying, 'Santa only brings toys to *good* boys and girls.' I stole a glance from Stan. There was sorrow in his eyes, and I could tell that he understood Mother's freakish games. Since I was still under punishment, on Christmas Day I had to change into my work clothes and perform my chores. While I was cleaning the bathroom, I overheard an argument between Mother and Father. She was angry with him for 'going behind her back' to buy me the paintings. Mother told Father that *she* was in charge of disciplining 'the boy' and that he had undermined her authority by buying the gifts. The longer Father argued his case, the angrier she became. I could tell he had lost, and that I was becoming more and more isolated.

A few months later, Mother became a den mother for the Cub Scouts. Whenever the other kids came to our home, she treated them like kings. Some of the other kids told me how they wished their mothers would be like mine. I never responded, but I wondered to myself what they would think if they knew the real truth. Mother only kept the den mother job for a few months. When she gave it up I was so relieved because it meant I could go to other kids' homes for the Wednesday meetings.

One Wednesday, I came home from school to change into my blue and gold Cub Scout uniform. Mother and I were the only ones in the house, and I could tell by the look on her face that she was after blood. After smashing my face against the bedroom mirror, she snatched my arm and dragged me to the car. During the drive to my den mother's house, Mother told me what she was going to do with me when we got home. I scooted to the far side of the front seat of the car, but it didn't work. She reached across the seat and seized my chin, lifting my head towards hers. Mother's eyes were bloodshot and her voice sounded as if she were possessed. When we arrived at the den mother's house, I ran to the door crying. I whined to her that I had been a bad boy and could not attend the meeting. The den mother smiled politely, saying that she would like me to come to the next meeting. That was the last time I saw her.

Once home, Mother ordered me to strip off my clothes and stand by the kitchen stove. I shook from a combination of fear and embarrassment. She then revealed my hideous crime. Mother told me that she had often driven to school to watch my brothers and I play during our lunch period recess. Mother claimed that she had seen me that very day playing on the grass, which was absolutely forbidden by her rules. I quickly answered that I never played on the grass. I knew Mother had somehow made a mistake. My reward for observing Mother's rules and telling the truth was a hard punch in the face.

Mother then reached over and turned on the gas burners to the kitchen stove. Mother told me that she had read an article about a mother who had her son lie on top of a hot stove. I instantly became terrified. My brain became numb, and my legs wobbled. I wanted to disappear. I closed my eyes, wishing her away. My brain locked up when I felt Mother's hand clamp my arm as if it were in a vice grip.

'You've made my life a living hell!' she sneered. 'Now it's time I showed *you* what hell is like!' Gripping my arm, Mother held it in the orange-blue flame. My skin seemed to explode from the heat. I could smell the scorched hairs from my burnt arm. As hard as I fought, I could not force Mother to let go of my arm. Finally I fell to the floor, on my hands and knees, and tried to blow cool air on my arm. 'It's too bad your drunken father's not here to save you,' she hissed. Mother then ordered me to climb up onto the stove and lie on the flames so she could watch me burn. I refused, crying and pleading. I felt so scared I stomped my feet in protest. But Mother continued to force me on top of the stove. I watched the flames, praying the gas might run out.

Suddenly I began to realize the longer I could keep myself off the top of the stove, the better my chances were for staying alive. I knew my brother Ron would soon be coming home from his scout meeting, and I knew Mother never acted this bizarre when anyone else was in the house. In order to survive, I had to buy time. I stole a glance at the kitchen clock behind me. The second hand seemed to creep ever so slowly. To keep Mother off balance, I began to ask whining questions. This infuriated her even more, and Mother began to rain blows around my head and chest. The more Mother slugged me, the more I began to realize I had won! Anything was better than burning on the stove.

Finally, I heard the front door fly open. It was Ron. My heart surged with relief. The blood from Mother's face drained. She knew she had lost. For a moment in time, Mother froze. I seized that instant to grab my clothes and race to the garage, where I quickly dressed. I stood against the wall and began to whimper until I realized that *I* had beaten her. *I* had bought a few precious minutes. *I* had used my head to survive. For the first time, *I* had won!

Standing alone in that damp, dark garage, I knew, for the first time, that I could survive. I decided that I would use any tactic I could think of to defeat Mother or to delay her from her grisly obsession. I knew if *I* wanted to live, *I* would have to think ahead. I could no longer cry like a helpless baby. In order to survive, *I* could never give in to her. That day I vowed to myself that I would never, ever again give that bitch the satisfaction of hearing me beg her to stop beating me.

In the coldness of the garage, my entire body trembled from both the cold anger and intense fear. I used my tongue to lick the burn and soothe my throbbing arm. I wanted to scream, but I refused to give Mother the pleasure of hearing me cry. *I* stood tall. I could hear Mother talking to Ron upstairs, telling him how proud she was of him, and how she didn't have to worry about Ron becoming like David – a bad boy.

Chapter 4
# The Fight for Food

The summer after the burn incident, school became my only hope of escape. Except for the short duration of a fishing trip, things with Mother were touch and go, or smash and dash – she would smash me, and I would dash to the solitude of the basement/garage. The month of September brought school and bliss. I had new clothes and a shiny, new lunch pail. Because Mother had me wear the same clothes week after week, by October my clothes had become weathered, torn and smelly. She hardly bothered to cover my bruises on my face and arms. When asked, I had my ready-made excuses Mother brainwashed into me.

By then, Mother would 'forget' to feed me any dinner. Breakfast wasn't much better. On a good day, I was allowed left-over cereal portions from my brothers, but only if I performed all of my chores before going to school.

At night I was so hungry, my stomach growled as if I were an angry bear. At night I lay awake concentrating on food. '*Maybe tomorrow I'll get dinner,*' I said to myself. Hours later, I would drift off to sleep, fantasizing about food. I mainly dreamed of colossal hamburgers with all the fixings. In my dreams I seized my prize and brought it to my lips, I visualized every inch of the hamburger. The meat dripped with grease, and thick slices of cheese bubbled on top. Condiments oozed between the lettuce and tomato. As I brought the hamburger closer to my face, I opened my mouth to devour my prize, but nothing happened. I'd try again and again, but no matter how hard I struggled, I could not taste a morsel of my fantasy. Moments later I would wake up, with my stomach more hollow than before. I could not satisfy my hunger; not even in my dreams.

Soon after I had begun to dream about food, I started stealing food at school. My stomach coiled with a combination of fear and anticipation. Anticipation because I knew that within seconds, I would have something to put in my stomach. Fear because I also knew that at any time, I could get caught stealing. I always stole food before school began, while my classmates were playing outside the building. I would sneak to the wall, right outside my homeroom, drop my lunch pail by another pail and kneel down so nobody could see me hunting through their lunches. The first few times were easy, but after several days, some students began to discover Twinkies and other deserts missing from their lunches. Within a short time, my classmates began to hate me. The teacher told the principal, who in turn informed Mother. The fight for food became a cycle. The principal's report to Mother led to more beatings and less food for me at the house.

On weekends, to punish me for my thefts, Mother refused to feed me. By Sunday night, my mouth would water as I began to plot new, fool-proof ways to steal food without getting caught. One of my plots was to steal from other first-grade rooms, where I wasn't known as well. On Monday mornings I would dash from Mother's car to a new first-grade classroom to pick through lunch boxes. I got away with it for a short time, but it didn't take long for the principal to trace the thefts back to me.

At the house, the dual punishment of hunger and

violent attacks continued. By this time, for all practical purposes, I was no longer a member of the family. I existed, but there was little or no recognition. Mother had even stopped using my name; referring to me only as The Boy. I was not allowed to eat meals with the family, play with my brothers, or watch television. I was grounded to the house. I was not allowed to look at or speak to anybody. When I returned to the house from school, I immediately accomplished the various chores Mother assigned me. When the chores were finished, I went directly to the basement, where I stood until summoned to clean off the dinner table and wash the dishes. It was made very clear that getting caught sitting or lying down in the basement would bring dire consequences. I had become Mother's slave.

Father was my only hope, and he did all he could to sneak me scraps of food. He tried to get Mother drunk, thinking the liquor might leave her in a better mood. He tried to get Mother to change her mind about feeding me. He even attempted to make deals, promising her the world. But all his attempts were useless. Mother was as solid as a rock. If anything, her drunkenness made it worse. Mother became more like a monster.

I knew Father's efforts to help me led to stress between he and Mother. Soon, midnight arguments began to occur. From bed I could hear the tempo build to an ear-shattering climax. By then they were both drunk, and I could hear Mother scream every vulgar phrase imaginable. It didn't matter what issue started the fight, I would soon be the object of their battle. I knew Father was trying to help, but in bed I still shivered with fear. I knew he would lose, making things worse for me the next day. When they first began to fight, Mother would storm off in the car with the tyres screeching. She usually returned home in less than an hour. The next day, they would both act as if nothing had happened. I was grateful when Father found an excuse to come down to the basement and sneak me a piece of bread. He always promised me he would keep trying.

As the arguments between Mother and Father became more frequent, he began to change. Often after an argument, he would pack an overnight bag and set off in the middle of the night for work. After he left, Mother would yank me out of bed and drag me to the kitchen. While I stood shivering in my pyjamas, she'd smack me from one side of the kitchen to the other. One of my resistance techniques was to lay on the floor acting as though I didn't have the strength to stand. That tactic didn't last long. Mother would yank me up by the ears and yell into my face with her bourbon breath, for minutes at a time. On these nights, her message was always the same: I was the reason she and Father were having problems. Often I became so tired, my legs would shake. My only escape was to stare at the floor and hope that Mother would soon run out of steam.

By the time I was in the second grade, Mother was pregnant with her fourth child. My teacher, Miss Moss, began to take a special interest in me. She began by questioning me about my attentiveness. I lied, saying I had stayed up late watching television. My lies were not convincing, and she continued to pry not only about why I was sleepy, but also about the condition of my clothes and the bruises on my body. Mother always coached me on what to say about my appearance, so I simply passed Mother's story to the teacher.

Months crept by and Miss Moss became more

persistent. One day, she finally reported her concerns to the school principal. He knew me well as the food thief, so he called Mother. When I returned to the house that day, it was as if somebody had dropped an atomic bomb. Mother was more violent than ever. She was furious that some 'Hippie' teacher had turned her in for child abuse. Mother said that she would meet with the principal by the next day to justify all the false accusations. By the end of the session, my nose bled twice and I was missing a tooth.

When I returned from school the next afternoon, Mother smiled as if she had won a million-dollar sweepstake. She told me how she had dressed up to see the principal, with her infant son Russell in her arms. Mother told me how she had explained to the principal how David had an overactive imagination. Mother told him how David had often struck and scratched himself to get attention, since the recent birth of his new brother, Russell. I could imagine her turning on her snake-like charm as she cuddled Russell for the benefit of the principal. At the end of their talk, Mother said that she was more than happy to cooperate with the school. She said they could call her any time there was a problem with David. Mother said the staff at school had been instructed to pay no attention to my wild stories of child beating or not being fed. Standing there in the kitchen that day, listening to her boast, gave me a feeling of total emptiness. As Mother told me about the meeting, I could sense her heightened confidence, and her new confidence made me fear for my life. I wished I could dissolve and be gone forever. I wished I would never have to face another human being again.

That summer, the family vacationed at the Russian River. Although I got along better with Mother, the magical feeling had disappeared. The hayrides, the weenie roasts and story telling were things of the past. We spent more and more time in the cabin. Even the day trips to Johnson's Beach were rare.

Father tried to make the vacation more fun by taking the three of us to play on the new super slide. Russell, who was still a toddler, stayed in the cabin with Mother. One day, when Ron, Stan and I were playing at a neighbor's cabin, Mother came out onto the porch and yelled for us to come in immediately. Once in the cabin, I was scolded for making too much noise. For my punishment, I was not allowed to go with Father and my brothers to the super slide. I sat on a chair in a corner, shivering, hoping that something would happen so the three of them wouldn't leave. I knew Mother had something hideous on her mind. As soon as they left, she brought out one of Russell's soiled diapers. She smeared the diaper on my face. I tried to sit perfectly still. I knew if I moved, it would only be worse. I didn't look up. I couldn't see Mother standing over me, but I could hear her heavy breathing.

After what seemed like an hour, Mother knelt down beside me and in a soft voice said, 'Eat it.'

I looked straight ahead, avoiding her eyes. '*No way!*' I said to myself. Like so many times before, avoiding her was the wrong thing to do. Mother smacked me from side to side. I clung to the chair, fearing if I fell off she would jump on me.

'I said eat it!' she sneered.

Switching tactics, I began to cry. '*Slow her down,*' I thought to myself. I began to count to myself, trying to concentrate. Time was my only ally. Mother answered my crying with more blows to my face, stopping only when she heard Russell crying.

Even with my face covered with defecation, I was pleased. I thought I might win. I tried to wipe the shit away, flicking it onto the wooden floor. I could hear Mother singing softly to Russell, and I imagined him cradled in her arms, I prayed he wouldn't fall asleep. A few minutes later my luck ran out.

Still smiling, Mother returned to her conquest. She grabbed me by the back of the neck and led me to the kitchen. There, spread out on the counter top, was another full diaper. The smell turned my stomach. 'Now, you are going to eat it!' she said. Mother had the same look in her eyes that she had the day she wanted me to lie on top of the gas stove back at the house. Without moving my head, I moved my eyes, searching for the daisy-colored clock that I knew was on the wall. A few seconds later, I realized the clock was behind me. Without the clock, I felt helpless. I knew I needed to lock my concentration on something, in order to keep any kind of control of the situation. Before I could find the clock, Mother's hands seized my neck. Again she repeated. 'Eat it!' I held my breath. The smell was overpowering. I tried to focus on the top corner of the diaper. Seconds seemed like hours. Mother must have known my plan. She slammed my face into the diaper and rubbed it from side to side.

I anticipated her move. As I felt my head being forced down, I closed my eyes tightly and clamped my mouth shut. My nose struck first. A warm sensation oozed from my nostrils. I tried to stop the blood from escaping by breathing in. I snorted bits of defecation back up my nose with the blood. I threw my hands on the counter top and tried to pull myself out of her grip. I twisted from side to side with all my strength, but she was too powerful. Suddenly Mother let go. 'They're back! They're back!' she gasped. Mother snatched a wash cloth from the sink and threw it at me. 'Clean the shit off your face,' she bellowed as she wiped the brown stains from the counter top. I wiped my face the best I could, but not before blowing bits of defecation from my nose. Moments later, Mother stuffed a piece of napkin up my bloody nose and ordered me to sit in the corner. I sat there for the rest of the evening, still smelling traces of the diaper through my nose.

The family never returned to the Russian River again.

In September, I returned to school with last year's clothes and my old, rusted, green lunch pail. I was a walking disgrace. Mother packed the same lunch for me every day: two peanut butter sandwiches and a few limp carrot sticks. Since I was no longer a member of the family, I was not allowed to ride to school in the family station wagon. Mother had me run to school. She knew I would not arrive in time to steal any food from my classmates.

At school I was a total outcast. No other kid would have anything to do with me. During the lunch recesses, I stuffed the sandwiches down my throat as I listened to my former friends make up songs about me. 'David the Food Thief' and 'Pelzer-Smellzer' were two of the playground favorites. I had no one to talk to or play with. I felt all alone.

At the house, while standing for hours in the garage, I passed the time by imagining new ways to feed myself. Father occasionally tried to sneak scraps of food to me, but with little success. I came to believe if I were to survive, *I* would have to rely on myself. I had exhausted all possibilities at school. All the students now hid their lunch pails, or locked them in the coat closet of the classroom. The teachers and principal knew me and carefully watched me. I had little to no chance of stealing any more food at school.

Finally, I devised a plan that might work. Students

were not allowed to leave the playground during lunch recess, so nobody would expect me to leave. My idea was to sneak away from the playground and run to the local grocery store, and steal cookies, bread, chips or whatever I could. In my mind, I planned every step of my scheme. When I ran to school the next morning, I counted every step so I could calculate my pace and later apply it to my trip to the store. After a few weeks, I had all the information I needed. The only thing left was finding the courage to attempt the plan. I knew it would take longer to go from the school to the store because it was up a hill, so I allowed 15 minutes. Coming back downhill would be easier, so I allowed 10 minutes. This meant I had only 10 minutes at the store.

Each day when I ran to and from school, I tried to run faster, pounding each step as if I were a marathon runner. As the days passed and my plan became more solid, my hunger for food was replaced by daydreaming. I fantasized whenever performing my chores at the house. On my hands and knees while scrubbing the bathroom tiles, I imagined I was the prince in the story 'The Prince and the Pauper'. As the Prince, I knew I could end the charade of acting like a servant any time I wanted. In the basement, I stood perfectly still with my eyes closed, dreaming I was a comic-book hero. But my daydream was always interrupted by hunger pangs, and my thoughts soon returned to my plan of stealing food.

Even when I was sure my plan was foolproof, I was too afraid to put it into action. During the lunch recess at school, I strolled around the playground making excuses to myself for my lack of guts to run to the store. I told myself I would get caught or that my timing calculations were not accurate. All through the argument with myself, my stomach growled, calling me a 'chicken'. Finally, after several days without dinner and only the small left-over portions for breakfast, I decided to do it. A few moments after the lunch bell rang, I blitzed up the street, away from the school, with my heart pounding and my lungs bursting for air. I made it to the store in half the time I allowed myself. Walking up and down the aisles of the store, I felt as if everybody was staring at me. I felt as though all the customers were talking about the smelly, ragged child. It was then that I knew my plan was doomed because I had not taken into account how I might look to other people. The more I worried about my appearance, the more my stomach became seized with fear. I froze in the aisle, not knowing what to do. I slowly began to count the seconds away. I began to think about all the times I had been starving. Suddenly without thinking, I grabbed the first thing I saw on the shelf, ran out of the store and raced back to school. Clutched tightly in my hand was my prize – a box of graham crackers.

As I came near the school I hid my possession under my shirt, on the side that didn't have any holes, as I walked through the schoolyard. Inside, I ditched the food in the garbage can of the boys' restroom. Later that afternoon, after making an excuse to the teacher, I returned to the restroom to devour my prize. I could feel my mouth begin to water, but my heart sank as I looked into an empty trash can. All my careful plans and all the pain of convincing myself that I would eat, were wasted. The custodian had emptied the trash can before I could slip away to the restroom.

That day my plan failed, but on other attempts I was lucky. Once, I managed to hide my treasure in my desk in homeroom, only to find on the next day that I had been transferred to the school across the street. Except for losing the stolen food, I welcomed the transfer. Now, I felt I had a new license to steal. Not only was I able to snitch food from my classmates again, but I also sprinted to the grocery store about once a week. Sometimes at the grocery store, if I felt things weren't just right, I didn't steal anything. As always, I finally got caught. The manager called Mother. At the house, I was thrashed relentlessly. Mother knew why I stole food and so did Dad, but she still refused to feed me. The more I craved food, the more I tried to come up with a better plan to steal it.

After dinner, it was Mother's habit to scrape the leftovers from the dinner plates into a small garbage can. Then she would summon me up from the basement, where I had been standing while the family ate. It was my function to wash the dishes. Standing there with my hands in the scalding water, I could smell the scraps from dinner in the small garbage can. At first my idea was nauseating, but the more I thought about it, the better it seemed. It was my only hope for food. I finished the dishes as fast as I could and emptied the garbage in the garage. My mouth watered at the sight of the food, and I gingerly picked the good pieces out while scraping bits of paper or cigarette butts away, and gobbled the food as fast as I could.

As usual, my new plan came to an abrupt halt when Mother caught me in the act. For a few weeks I quit the garbage routine, but I finally had to return to it, in order to silence my growling stomach. Once, I ate some left-over pork. Hours later I was bent over in extreme pain. I had diarrhea for a week. While I was sick, Mother informed me she had purposefully left the meat in the refrigerator for two weeks, to spoil before she threw it away. She knew I couldn't resist stealing it. As time progressed, Mother had me bring the garbage can to her so she could inspect it while she lay on the couch. She never knew that I wrapped food between paper towels and hid them in the bottom of the can. I knew she wouldn't want to get her fingers dirty, digging in the bottom of the trash can, so my scheme worked for a while.

Mother sensed I was getting food some way, so she began sprinkling ammonia in the trash can. After that, I gave up on the garbage at the house and focused my sights on finding some other way to get food at school. After getting caught stealing from other kids' lunches, my next idea was to rip off frozen lunches from the school cafeteria.

I timed my restroom break so that the teacher excused me from the classroom just after the delivery truck dropped off its supply of frozen lunches. I crept into the cafeteria and snatched a few frozen trays, then I scurried to the restroom. Alone in the restroom, I swallowed the frozen hot dogs and tater tots in huge chunks so fast I almost choked myself in the process. After filling my stomach I returned to the classroom, feeling so proud *I* fed myself.

As I ran to the house from school that afternoon, all I could think about was stealing food from the cafeteria the next day. Minutes later, Mother changed my mind. She dragged me into the bathroom and slugged me in the stomach so hard that I bent over. Pulling me around to face the toilet, she ordered me to shove my finger down my throat. I resisted. I tried my old trick of counting to myself, as I stared into the porcelain toilet bowl, 'One . . . two . . .' I never made it to three. Mother rammed her finger into my mouth, as if she wanted to pull my stomach up through my throat. I squirmed in every direction in an effort to fight her. She finally let me go, but only when I agreed that I would vomit for her.

I knew what was going to happen next. I closed my eyes as chunks of red meat spilled into the toilet. Mother just stood behind me, with her hands on her hips and said, 'I thought so. Your Father's going to hear about this!' I tensed myself for the volley of blows that I knew was coming, but nothing happened. After a few seconds, I spun around to discover that Mother had left the bathroom. I knew the episode wasn't over. Moments later she returned with a small bowl, ordered me to scoop the partially-digested food out of the toilet and put it in the bowl. Since Father was away shopping at the time, Mother was gathering evidence for his return.

Later that night, after I finished all of my evening chores, Mother had me stand by the kitchen table while she and Father talked in the bedroom. In front of me was the bowl of hot dogs that I had vomited. I couldn't look at it, so I closed my eyes and tried to imagine myself far away from the house. A short time later, Mother and Father stormed into the kitchen. 'Look at this, Steve,' Mother barked, thrusting her finger in the direction of the bowl. 'So you think The Boy is through stealing food, do you?'

By the look on Father's face, I could tell he was getting more and more tired of the constant 'What has The Boy done now?' routine. Staring at me, he shook his head in disapproval and stammered, 'Well, Roerva, if you would just let The Boy have *something* to eat.'

A heated battle of words broke out in front of me, and as always, Mother won. 'EAT? You want The Boy to eat, Stephen? Well, The Boy is going to EAT! He can eat this!' Mother yelled at the top of her lungs, shoving the bowl towards me and stomping off to the bedroom.

The kitchen became so quiet I could hear Father's strained breathing. He gently placed his hand on my shoulder and said, 'Wait there, Tiger. I'll see what I can do.' He returned a few minutes later, after trying to talk Mother out of her demand. By the saddened look on his face, I knew immediately who'd won.

I sat on a chair and picked the clumps of hot dogs out of the bowl with my hand. Globs of thick saliva slipped through my fingers, as I dropped it in my mouth. As I tried to swallow, I began to whimper. I turned to Father, who stood looking through me with a drink in his hand. He nodded for me to continue. I couldn't believe he just stood there as I ate the revolting contents of the bowl. At that moment, I knew we were slipping further and further apart.

I tried to swallow without tasting, until I felt a hand clamp on the back of my neck. 'Chew it!' Mother snarled, 'Eat it! Eat it all!' she said, pointing to the saliva. I sat deeper in my chair. A river of tears rolled down my cheeks. After I had chewed the mess in the bowl, I tilted my head back and forced what remained, down my throat. I closed my eyes and screamed to myself to keep it from coming back up into my mouth. I didn't open my eyes until I was sure my stomach wasn't going to reject my cafeteria meal. When I did open them, I stared at Father who turned away to avoid my pain. At that moment I hated Mother to no end, but I hated Father even more. The man who had helped me in the past, just stood like a statue while his son ate something even a dog wouldn't touch.

After I finished the bowl of regurgitated hot dogs, Mother returned in her robe and threw a wad of newspapers at me. She informed me the papers were my blankets, and the floor under the table was now my bed. Again I shot a glance at Father, but he acted as though I was not even in the room. Forcing myself not to cry in front of them, I crawled, completely dressed, under the table, and covered myself with the newspapers, like a rat in a cage.

For months I slept under the breakfast table next to a box of kitty litter, but I soon learned to use the newspapers to my advantage. With the papers wrapped around me, my body heat kept me warm. Finally, Mother told me that I was no longer privileged enough to sleep upstairs, so I was banished downstairs to the garage. My bed was now an old army cot. To stay warm, I tried to keep my head close to the gas heater. But after a few cold nights, I found it best to keep my hands clamped under my arms and feet curled towards my buttocks. Sometimes at night I would wake up and try to imagine I was a real person, sleeping under a warm electric blanket, knowing I was safe and that somebody loved me. My imagination worked for awhile, but the cold nights always brought me back to my reality. I knew no one could help me. Not my teachers, my so-called brothers or even Father. I was on my own, and every night I prayed to God that I could be strong both in body and soul. In the darkness of the garage, I laid on the wooden cot and shivered until I fell into a restless sleep.

Once, during my midnight fantasies, I came up with the idea of begging for food on my way to school. Even though the after-school vomit inspection was carried out every day when I returned to the house from school, I thought that any food I ate in the morning would be digested by the afternoon. As I began my run to school, I made sure I ran extra fast so I would have more time for my hunt for food. I then altered my course – stopping and knocking on doors. I would ask the lady who answered if she happened to find a lunch box near her house. For the most part, my plan worked. I could tell by looking at these ladies that they felt sorry for me. Thinking ahead, I used a fake name so nobody would know who I really was. For weeks my plan worked, until one day when I came to the house of a lady who knew Mother. My time-tested story, 'I lost my lunch. Could you make me one?' fell apart. Even before I left her house, I knew she would call Mother.

That day at school I prayed for the world to end. As I fidgeted in the classroom, I knew Mother was lying on the couch, watching television and getting more drunk by the hour, while thinking of something hideous to do to me when I arrived at *her* house after school. Running to the house from school that afternoon, my feet felt as though they were encased in blocks of cement. With every step I prayed that Mother's friend had not called her, or had somehow mistaken me for another kid. Above me the skies were blue, and I could feel the sun's rays warm my back. As I approached Mother's house, I looked up towards the sun, wondering if I would ever see it again. I carefully cracked the front door open before slipping inside, and tiptoed down the stairs to the garage. I expected Mother to fly down the stairs and beat me on the cement floor any second. She didn't come. After changing into my work clothes, I crept upstairs to the kitchen and began washing Mother's lunch dishes. Not knowing where she might be, my ears became radar antennae, seeking out her exact location. As I washed the dishes, my back became tense with fear. My hands shook, and I couldn't concentrate on my chores. Finally, I heard Mother come out of her bedroom and walk down the hall towards the kitchen. For a fleeting moment I looked out of the window. I could hear the laughter and screams of the children playing. For a moment I closed my eyes and imagined I was one of them. I felt warm inside. I smiled.

My heart skipped a beat when I felt Mother breathing down my neck. Startled, I dropped a dish, but before it could hit the floor I snatched it out of the air. 'You're a quick little shit, aren't you?' she sneered. 'You can run fast and find time to beg for food. Well ... we'll just see how fast you really are.' Expecting Mother to bash me, I tensed my body, waiting for her to strike. When it didn't happen, I thought she would leave and return to her TV show, but that didn't happen either. Mother remained inches behind me, watching my every move. I could see her reflection in the kitchen window. Mother saw it too, and smiled back. I nearly peed my pants.

When I finished the dishes, I began cleaning the bathroom. Mother sat on the toilet as I scoured the bathtub. While I was on my hands and knees scrubbing the tile floor, she calmly and quietly stood behind me. I expected her to come around and kick me in the face, but she didn't. As I continued my chores, my anxiety grew. I knew Mother was going to beat me, but I didn't know how, when or where. It seemed to take forever for me to finish the bathroom.

By the time I did, my legs and arms were shaking with anticipation. I could not concentrate on anything but her. Whenever I found the courage to look up at Mother, she smiled and said, 'Faster young man. You'll have to move much faster than that.'

By dinner time, I was exhausted with fear. I almost fell asleep as I waited for Mother to summon me to clear the table and wash the evening dishes. Standing alone downstairs in the garage, my insides became unglued. I so badly wanted to run upstairs and go to the bathroom, but I knew without Mother's permission to move, I was a prisoner. *'Maybe that is what she has planned for me,'* I told myself. *'Maybe she wants me to drink my own pee.'* At first the thought was too crude to imagine, but I knew *I* had to be prepared to deal with anything Mother might throw at me. The more I tried to focus on my options of what she might do to me, the more my inner strength drained away. Then an idea flashed in my brain; I knew why Mother had followed every step I took. She wanted to maintain a constant pressure on me, by leaving me unsure of when or where she would strike. Before I could think of a way to defeat her. Mother bellowed me upstairs. In the kitchen she told me that only the speed of light would save me, so I had better wash the dishes in record time. 'Of course,' she sneered, 'there's no need to tell you that you're going without dinner tonight, but not to worry, I have a cure for your hunger.'

After finishing the evening chores, Mother ordered me to wait downstairs. I stood with my back against the hard wall, wondering what plans she had for me. I had no idea. I broke out in a cold sweat that seemed to seep through to my bones. I became so tired I fell asleep while standing. When I felt my head roll forward, I snapped it upright, waking myself. No matter how hard I tried to stay awake, I couldn't control my head that bobbed up and down like a piece of cork in water. While in my trance-like state, I could feel the strain lift my soul away from my body, as if I, too, were floating. I felt as light as a feather until my head rolled forward again, jolting me awake. I knew better than to fall into a deep slumber. To get caught could be deadly, so I escaped by staring through the molded garage window, listening to the sounds of the cars driving by and watching the red flashes of planes flying overhead. From the bottom of my heart I wished that I could fly away.

—

Hours later, after Ron and Stan went to bed, Mother ordered me to return upstairs. I dreaded every step. I knew the time had come. She had drained me emotionally and physically. I didn't know what she had planned. I simply wished Mother would beat me and get it over with.

As I opened the door, a calmness filled my soul. The house was dark except for a single light in the kitchen. I could see Mother sitting by the breakfast table. I stood completely still. She smiled, and I could tell by her slumped shoulders that the booze had her in a deep-six. In a strange way, I knew she wasn't going to beat me. My thoughts became cloudy, but my trance broke when Mother got up and strolled over to the kitchen sink. She knelt down, opened the sink cabinet and removed a bottle of ammonia. I didn't understand. She got a tablespoon and poured some ammonia into it. My brain was too rattled to think. As much as I wanted to, I could not get my numbed brain into gear.

With the spoon in her hand, Mother began to creep towards me. As some of the ammonia sloshed from the spoon, spilling onto the floor, I backed away from Mother until my head struck the counter top by the stove. I almost laughed inside. '*That's all? That's it? All she's going to do is have me swallow some of this?*' I said to myself.

I wasn't afraid. I was too tired. All I could think was, '*Come on, let's go. Let's get it over with.*' As Mother bent down, she again told me that only speed would save me. I tried to understand her puzzle, but my mind was too cloudy.

Without hesitation I opened my mouth, and Mother rammed the cold spoon deep into my throat. Again I told myself this was all too easy, but a moment later I couldn't breathe. My throat seized. I stood wobbling in front of Mother, feeling as if my eyes were going to pop out of my skull. I fell on the floor, on my hands and knees. '*Bubble!*' my brain screamed. I pounded the kitchen floor with all my strength, trying to swallow, and trying to concentrate on the bubble of air stuck in my esophagus. Instantly I became terrified. Tears of panic streamed down my cheeks. After a few seconds, I could feel the force of my pounding fists weaken. My fingernails scraped the floor. My eyes became fixed on the floor. The colors seemed to run together. I began to feel myself drift away. I knew I was going to die.

I came to my senses, and felt Mother slapping me on the back. The force of her blows made me burp, and I was able to breathe again. As I forced huge gulps of air back into my lungs, Mother returned to her glass of booze. She took a long drink, gazed down at me and blew a mist of air in my direction. 'Now, that wasn't so hard, was it?' Mother said, finishing her glass before dismissing me downstairs to my cot.

The next evening was a repeat performance, but this time in front of Father. She boasted to him, 'This will teach The Boy to quit stealing food!' I knew she was only doing it for her sick, perverted pleasure. Father stood lifeless as Mother fed me another dose of ammonia. But this time, I fought back. She had to pry my mouth open, and by thrashing my head from side to side, *I* was able to make her spill most of the cleaner onto the floor. But not enough. Again I clenched my fingers together, beating the floor. I looked up at Father, trying to call out to him. My thoughts were clear, but no sound escaped from my mouth. He simply stood above me, showing no emotion, as I pounded my hands by my feet. As if she were kneeling to pet one of her dogs, Mother again slapped me on the back a few times before I blacked out.

## The Fight for Food

The next morning while cleaning the bathroom, I looked in the mirror to inspect my burning tongue. Layers of flesh were scraped away, while remaining parts were red and raw. I stood, staring into the sink, feeling how lucky I was to be alive.

Although Mother never made me swallow ammonia again, she did make me drink spoonfuls of Clorox a few times. But Mother's favorite game seemed to be dish-washing soap. From the bottle she would squeeze the cheap, pink liquid down my throat and command that I stand in the garage. My mouth became so dry, I sneaked away to the garage faucet and filled my stomach full of water. Soon I discovered my dreadful mistake, and diarrhea took hold. I cried out to Mother upstairs, begging her to let me use the toilet upstairs. She refused. I stood downstairs, afraid to move, as clumps of the watery matter fell through my under-wear and down my pant legs, onto the floor.

I felt so degraded; I cried like a baby. I had no self-respect of any kind. I needed to go to the bathroom again, but I was too afraid to move. Finally, as my insides twisted and turned, I gathered the last of my dignity. I waddled to the garage sink, grabbed a five-gallon bucket and squatted to relieve myself. I closed my eyes trying to think of a way to clean myself and my clothes when suddenly, the garage door opened behind me. I turned my head to see Father, looking on dispassionately, as his son 'mooned' him and as the brown seepage spilled into the bucket. I felt lower than a dog.

Mother didn't always win. Once, during a week when I was not allowed to attend school, she squeezed the soap into my mouth and told me to clean the kitchen. She didn't know, but I refused to swallow the soap. As the minutes passed, my mouth became filled with a combination of soap and saliva. *I* would not allow myself to swallow. When I finished the kitchen chores, I raced downstairs to empty the trash. I smiled from ear to ear, as I closed the door behind me and spit out the mouthful of pink soap. At the trash cans by the garage door, I reached into one of the cans and plucked out a used paper towel, and wiped out the inside of my mouth ensuring that I removed every drop of soap. After I finished, I felt as though I had won the Olympic Marathon. I was so proud for beating Mother at her own game.

Even though Mother caught me in most of my attempts to feed myself, she couldn't catch me *all* the time. After months of being confined for hours at a time in the garage, my courage took over and I stole bits of frozen food from the garage freezer, I was fully aware that I could pay for my crime at any time, so I ate every morsel as if it were my last meal.

In the darkness of the garage I closed my eyes, dreaming I was a king dressed in the finest robes, eating the best food mankind had to offer. As I held a piece of frozen pumpkin pie crust or a bit of a taco shell, *I* was the king, and like a king on his throne, I gazed down on my food and smiled.

Chapter 5

# The Accident

The summer of 1971 set the tone for the remainder of the time that I lived with Mother.

I had not reached my 11th birthday, but for the most part, I knew what forms of punishment to expect. To exceed one of Mother's time limits on any of my multiple chores, meant no food. If I looked at her or one of her sons without her permission, I received a slap in the face. If I was caught stealing food, I knew Mother would either repeat an old form of punishment or dream up something new and hideous. Most of the time Mother seemed to know exactly what she was doing, and I could anticipate what she might do next. However, I always kept my guard up and tensed my entire body if I thought she might come my way.

As June turned to early July, my morale dwindled. Food was little more than a fantasy. I rarely received even left-over breakfast, no matter how hard I worked, and I was *never* fed lunch. As for dinner, I averaged about one evening meal every three days.

One particular July day began like any other mundane day, in my now slave-like existence. I had not eaten in three days. Because school was out for the summer, my options for finding food vanished. As always during dinner, I sat at the bottom of the stairs with my buttocks on top of my hands, listening to the sounds of 'the family' eating. Mother now demanded that I sit on my hands with my head thrust backward, in a 'prisoner of war' position. I let my head fall forward, half dreaming that I was one of them – a member of 'the family'. I must have fallen asleep because I was suddenly awakened by Mother's snarling voice, 'Get up here! Move your ass!' she yelled.

At the first syllable of her order I snapped my head level, stood up and sprinted up the stairs. I prayed that tonight I would get something, anything, to soothe my hunger.

I had begun clearing the dishes from the dining room table at a feverish pace, when Mother called me into the kitchen. I bowed my head as she began to babble her time limits to me. 'You have 20 minutes!

One minute, one second more, and you go hungry again! Is that understood?'

'Yes, ma'am.'

'Look at me when I'm talking to you!' she snapped.

Obeying her command, I slowly raised my head. As my head came up, I saw Russell rocking back and forth on Mother's left leg. The harsh tone of Mother's voice didn't seem to bother him. He simply stared at me through a set of cold eyes. Even though Russell was only four or five years old at the time, he had become Mother's 'Little Nazi', watching my every move, making sure I didn't steal my food. Sometimes he would make up tales for Mother so he could watch me receive punishment. It really wasn't Russell's fault. I knew Mother had brainwashed him, but I had begun to turn cold towards him and hate him just the same.

'Do you hear me?' Mother yelled. 'Look at me when I'm talking to you!' As I looked at her, Mother snatched a carving knife from the counter top and screamed, 'If you don't finish on time, I'm going to kill you!'

Her words had no effect on me. She had said the same thing over and over again for almost a week now. Even Russell wasn't fazed by her threat. He kept rocking on Mother's leg as if he were riding a stick pony. She apparently wasn't pleased with her renewed tactic because she continued to badger on and on as the clock ticked away, eating up my time limit. I wished she would just shut up and let me work. I was desperate to meet her time limits. I wanted so much to have something to eat. I dreaded going to sleep another night.

Something looked wrong. Very wrong! I strained to focus my eyes on Mother. She had begun to wave the knife in her right hand. Again, I was not overly frightened. She had done this before too. '*Eyes*,' I told myself. '*Look at her eyes*.' I did, and they seemed normal for her – half-glazed over. But my instincts told me there was something wrong. I didn't think she was going to hit me, but my body began to tense anyway. As I became more tense, I saw what was wrong. Partly because of Russell's rocking motion, and partly because of the motion of her arm and hand with the knife, Mother's whole body began to weave back and forth. For a moment I thought she was going to fall.

She tried to regain her balance, snapping at Russell to let go of her leg, while she continued to scream at me. By then, her upper body looked like a rocking chair that was out of control. Forgetting about her useless threats, I imagined that the old drunk was going to fall flat on her face. I focused all of my attention on Mother's face. Out of the corner of my eye I saw a blurred object fly from her hand. A sharp pain erupted from just above my stomach. I tried to remain standing, but my legs gave out, and my world turned black.

As I gained consciousness, I felt a warm sensation flowing from my chest. It took me a few seconds to realize where I was. I sat propped up on the toilet. I turned towards Russell who began chanting, 'David's going to die. The Boy's going to die.' I moved my eyes towards my stomach. On her knees, Mother was hastily applying a thick wad of gauze to a place on my stomach where dark red blood pumped out. I tried to say something. I knew it was an accident. I wanted Mother to know that I forgave her, but I felt too faint to speak. My head slumped forward again and again, as I tried to hold it up. I lost track of time as I returned to darkness.

When I woke up, Mother was still on her knees wrapping a cloth around my lower chest. She knew exactly what she was doing. Many times when we were younger, Mother told Ron, Stan and I how she had intended to become a nurse, until she met Father. Whenever she was confronted with an accident around the home, she was in complete control. I never doubted her nursing abilities for a second. I simply waited for her to load me in the car and take me to the hospital. I felt that she would. It was just a matter of time. I felt a curious sense of relief. I knew in my heart it was over. This whole charade of living like a slave had come to an end. Even Mother could not lie about this one. I felt the accident had set me free.

It took Mother nearly half an hour to dress my wound. There was no remorse in her eyes. I thought that, at the very least, she would try to comfort me with her soothing voice. Looking at me with no emotion, Mother stood up, washed her hands and told me I now had 30 minutes to finish the dishes. I shook my head, trying to understand what she had said. After a few seconds, Mother's message sunk in. Just as in the arm incident a few years ago. Mother was not going to acknowledge what had happened.

I had no time for self-pity. The clock was running. I stood up, wobbled for a few seconds, then made my way to the kitchen. With every step, pain ripped through my ribs and blood seeped through my ragged T-shirt. By the time I reached the kitchen sink, I leaned over and panted like an old dog.

From the kitchen I could hear Father in the living room, flipping through his newspaper. I took a painfully deep breath, hoping that I could shove off and make my way to Dad. But I breathed too hard, and fell to the floor. After that I realized I had to take short, choppy breaths. I made my way into the living room. Sitting on the far end of the couch was my hero. I knew he would take care of Mother and drive me to the hospital. I stood before Father, waiting for him to turn his page and see me. When he did, I stuttered, 'Father . . . Mo . . . Mo . . . Mother stabbed me.'

He didn't even raise an eyebrow. 'Why?' he asked.

'She told me if I didn't do the dishes on time . . . she'd kill me.'

Time stood still. From behind the paper I could hear Father's labored breathing. He cleared his throat before saying, 'Well . . . you ah . . . you better go back in there and do the dishes.' My head leaned forward as if to catch his words. I couldn't believe what I had just heard. Father must have sensed my confusion when I saw him snap his paper and heard him raise his voice saying, 'Jesus H. Christ! Does Mother know that you're here talking to me? You better go back in there, and do the dishes. Damn it boy, we don't need to do anything that might make her more upset! I don't need to go through that tonight . . .' Father stopped for a second, took a deep breath and lowered his voice, whispering, 'I tell you what; you go back in there and do the dishes. I won't even tell her that you told, okay? This will be *our* little secret. Just go back in the kitchen and do the dishes. Go on now, before she catches the both of us. Go!'

I stood before Father in total shock. He didn't even look at me. Somehow I felt if he could at least turn a corner flap of the paper and search into my eyes, he would know; he would feel my pain, how desperate I was for his help. But, as always, I knew that Mother controlled him like she controlled everything that happened in her house. I think Father and I both knew the code of 'the family' – if we don't acknowledge a problem, it simply does not exist. As I stood before Father, not knowing what to do next, I looked down and saw droplets of blood staining the family's carpet. I had felt in my heart that he would scoop me up in his arms and take me away. I even imagined him ripping off his shirt to expose his true identity, before flying through the air like Superman.

I turned away. All my respect for Father was gone. The savior I had imagined for so long was a phony. I felt more angry at him than I did at Mother. I wished that somehow I could fly away, but the throbbing pain brought me back to reality.

I washed the dishes as fast as my body would let me. I quickly learned that moving my forearm resulted in a sharp pain above my stomach. If I sidestepped from the wash basin to the rinse basin, another pain raced through my body. I could feel what little strength I had, draining away. As Mother's time limit passed, so did my chances of getting fed.

I wanted to just lie down and quit, but the promise I made years ago kept me going. I wanted to show The Bitch that she could beat me only if I died, and I was determined not to give in, even to death. As I washed the dishes, I learned that by standing on my toes and leaning my upper body towards the counter top, I could relieve some of the pressure on my lower chest. Instead of sidestepping every few seconds, I washed a few dishes at a time, then moved over and rinsed them all together. After drying the dishes, I dreaded the task of putting them away. The cupboards were above my head, and I knew reaching for them would cause great pain. Holding a small plate, I stretched my legs as far as I could and tried to raise my arms above my head to put the dish away. I almost made it, but the pain was too great. I crumpled to the floor.

By now, my shirt was saturated with blood. As I tried to regain my footing. I felt Father's strong hands helping me. I brushed him away. 'Give me the dishes,' he said. 'I'll put them away. You better go downstairs and change that shirt.' I didn't say a word as I turned away. I looked at the clock. It had taken me nearly an hour and a half to complete my chore. My right hand clamped tightly onto the railing, as I slowly made my way downstairs. I could actually see the blood seep from my T-shirt with every step I took.

Mother met me at the bottom of the stairs. As she tore the shirt from my body, I could see Mother was doing it as gently as she could, however, she gave me no other comfort. I could see it was just a matter of business to her. In the past, I had seen her treat animals with more compassion than she did me.

I was so weak that I accidentally fell against her as

she dressed me in an old, oversized T-shirt. I expected Mother to hit me, but she allowed me to rest against her for a few seconds. Then Mother set me at the bottom of the stairs and left. A few minutes later, Mother returned with a glass of water. I gulped it down as fast as I could swallow. When I finished, Mother told me that she couldn't feed me right away. She said she would feed me in a few hours when I felt better. Again, her voice was monotone – completely without emotion.

Stealing a glance, I could see the California twilight being overtaken by darkness. Mother told me I could play outside with the boys, on the driveway in front of the garage door. My head was not clear. It took me a few seconds to understand what she had said. 'Go on, David. Go,' she persisted. With Mother's help, I limped out of the garage to the driveway. My brothers casually looked me over, but they were much more interested in lighting their Fourth-of-July sparklers. As the minutes passed, Mother became more compassionate towards me. She held me by the shoulders as we watched my brothers make figures eight with their sparklers. 'Would you like one?' Mother asked. I nodded yes. She held my hand as she knelt down to light the sparkler. For a moment, I imagined the scent of the perfume Mother wore years ago. But she had not used perfume or made up her face for a long time.

As I played with my brothers, I couldn't help but think about Mother and the change in the way she was treating me. '*Is she trying to make up with me?*' I wondered. '*Are my days living in the basement finally over? Am I back in the family fold?*' For a few minutes I didn't care. My brothers seemed to accept my presence, and I felt a feeling of friendship and warmth with them that I thought had been buried forever.

Within a few seconds my sparkler fizzled out. I turned towards the retreating sun. It had been forever since I had watched a sunset. I closed my eyes, trying to soak up as much heat as I could. For a few fleeting moments my pain, my hunger and my miserable way of life disappeared. I felt so warm, so alive. I opened my eyes, hoping to capture the moment for the rest of eternity.

Before she went to bed, Mother gave me more water and fed me some small bites of food. I felt like a disabled animal being nursed back to health, but I didn't care.

Downstairs in the garage I laid on my old army cot.

I tried not to think of the pain, but it was impossible to ignore as it crept throughout my body. Finally exhaustion took over and I drifted off to sleep. During the night I had several nightmares. I startled myself, waking up in a cold sweat. Behind me I heard a sound that scared me. It was Mother. She bent down and applied a cold wash cloth to my forehead. She told me that I had been running a fever during the night. I was too tired and weak to respond. All I could think about was the pain. Later, Mother returned to my brothers' downstairs bedroom, which was closer to the garage. I felt safe knowing she was nearby to watch over me.

Soon I drifted back into darkness, and with the fitful sleep came a dreadful dream of sheets of red, hot rain. In the dream I seemed to drench in it. I tried wiping the blood off my body only to find it quickly covered again. When I awoke the next morning, I stared at my hands which were crusted with dried blood. The shirt covering my chest was entirely red. I could feel the dried blood on parts of my face. I heard the bedroom door behind me open, and I turned to see Mother walking towards me. I expected more sympathy like she had given me the night before, but it was an empty hope. She gave me nothing. In a cold voice, Mother told me to clean myself up and begin my chores. As I heard her march up the stairs, I knew nothing had changed. I was still the bastard of the family.

About three days after the 'accident', I continued to feel feverish. I didn't dare ask Mother for even an aspirin, especially since Father was away at work. I knew she was back to her normal self. I thought the fever was due to my injury. The slit in my stomach had opened up more than once since that night. Quietly, so Mother wouldn't hear me, I crept to the garage sink. I picked up the cleanest rag I could find in my heap of rags. I cracked the water faucet open just enough to let a few drops of water spill onto the rag. Then I sat down and rolled up my red, soggy shirt. I touched my wound, flinching from the pain. I took a deep breath and as gently as possible, pinched the slit. The pain was so bad I threw my head back against the cold concrete floor, amost knocking myself out. When I looked at my stomach again, I saw a yellowish-white substance begin to ooze from the red, angry slash. I didn't know much about such things, but I knew it was infected. I started to get up to go upstairs and ask Mother to clean me up. When I was half-standing, I stopped. '*No!*' I told myself. '*I don't need that bitch's help.*' I knew enough about basic first-aid training to clean a wound, so I felt confident that I could do it alone. I wanted to be in charge of myself. I didn't want to rely on Mother or give her any more control over me than she already had.

I wet the rag again and brought it down towards my wound. I hesitated before I touched it. My hands were shaking with fear, as tears streamed down my face. I felt like a baby and hated it. Finally I told myself, '*You cry, you die. Now take care of the wound.*' I realized that my injury probably wasn't life-threatening; I brainwashed myself to block out the pain.

I moved quickly before my motivation slipped away. I snatched another rag, rolled it up and stuffed it into my mouth. I focused all my attention on the thumb and first finger of my left hand, as I pinched the skin around my slit. With my other hand I wiped away the pus. I repeated the process until blood seeped through, and I was wiping away only blood. Most of the white stuff was gone. The pain from the pinching and wiping was more than I could stand. With my teeth clamped tightly on the rag, my screaming was muffled. I felt as though I was hanging from a cliff. By the time I finished, a river of tears soaked the neck of my shirt.

Fearing Mother would catch me not sitting at the bottom of the stairs, I cleaned up my mess then half-walked, half-crawled to my assigned place at the foot of the staircase. Before I sat on my hands, I checked my shirt; only small drops of blood escaped from the wound to the rag bandage. I willed the wound to heal. Somehow I knew it would. I felt proud of myself. I imagined myself like a character in a comic book, who overcame great odds and survived. Soon my head slumped forward and I fell asleep. In my dream, I flew through the air in vivid colors. I wore a cape of red ... I was Superman.

Chapter 6

# While Father Is Away

After the knife incident, Father spent less and less time at home and more at work. He made excuses to the family, but I didn't believe him. I often shivered with fear as I sat in the garage, hoping for some reason he might not leave. In spite of all that had happened, I still felt Father was my protector. When he was home, Mother only did about half the things to me that she did when he was gone.

When Father was home, it became his habit to help me with the evening dishes. Father washed and I dried. While we worked, we talked softly so neither Mother nor the other boys could hear us. Sometimes, several minutes would pass without us talking. We wanted to make sure the coast was clear.

Father always broke the ice. 'How ya doin', Tiger?' he would say.

Hearing the old name that Father used when I was a little boy, always brought a smile to my face. 'I'm OK,' I would answer.

'Did you have anything to eat today?' he often asked. I usually shook my head in a negative gesture.

'Don't worry,' he'd say. 'Some day you and I will both get out of this madhouse.'

I knew father hated living at home, and I felt that it was all my fault. I told him that I would be good and that I wouldn't steal food anymore. I told Father I would try harder and do a better job on my chores. When I said these things, he always smiled and assured me that it wasn't my fault.

Sometimes as I dried the dishes, I felt a new ray of hope. I knew Father probably wouldn't do anything against Mother, but when I stood beside him I felt safe.

Like all good things that happened to me, Mother put an end to Father helping me with the dishes. She insisted that The Boy needed no help. She said that Father paid too much attention to me and not enough to others in the family. Without a fight, Father gave up. Mother now had complete control over everybody in the household.

After awhile, Father didn't even stay home on his days off. He would come in for only a few minutes. After seeing my brothers, he would find me wherever I was doing my chores and say a few sentences, then leave. It took Father no more than 10 minutes to get in and out of the house, and be on his way back to his solitude, which he usually found in a bar. When Father talked to me, he'd tell me that he was making plans for the two of us to leave. This always made me smile, but deep inside I knew it was a fantasy.

One day, he knelt down to tell me how sorry he was. I looked into his face. The change in Father frightened me. He had dark black circles around his eyes, and his face and neck were beet red. Father's once rigid shoulders were now slumped over. Gray had begun to take over his jet-black hair. Before he left that day, I threw my arms around his waist. I didn't know when I would see him again.

After finishing my chores that day, I rushed downstairs. I had been ordered to wash my ragged clothes and another heap of smelly rags. But that day, Father's leaving had left me so sad that I buried myself in the pile of rags and cried. I cried for him to come back and take me away. After a few minutes of self-comfort, I settled down and began scrubbing my 'Swiss cheese' clothes. I scrubbed until my knuckles bled. I no longer cared about my existence. Mother's house had become unbearable. I wished I could somehow manage to escape the place I now called the 'Madhouse'.

During one period of time when Father was away, Mother starved me for about ten consecutive days. No matter how hard I tried to meet her time limits, I couldn't make it. And the consequence was no food. Mother was completely thorough in making sure I was unable to steal any food. She cleared the dinner table herself, putting the food down the garbage disposal. She rummaged through the garbage can every day before I emptied it downstairs. She locked the freezer in the garage with her key and kept it. I was used to going without food for periods up to three days, but this extended time was unbearable. Water was my only means of survival. When I filled the metal ice cube tray from the refrigerator, I would tip the corner of the tray to my mouth. Downstairs I would creep to the wash basin and crack the faucet tap open. Praying that the pipe would not vibrate and alert Mother, I would carefully suck on the cold metal until my stomach was so full I thought it would burst.

By the sixth day I was so weak when I woke up on my army cot, I could hardly get up. I worked on my chores at a snail's pace. I felt so numb. My thought responses became unclear. It seemed to take minutes for me to understand each sentence Mother yelled to me. As I slowly strained my head up to look at Mother, I could tell that to her it was a game – a game which she thoroughly enjoyed.

'Oh, poor little baby,' Mother sarcastically cooed. Then she asked me how I felt, and laughed when I begged for food. At the end of the sixth day, and those that followed, I hoped with all my heart that Mother would feed me something, anything. I was at a point that I didn't care what it was.

One evening, towards the end of her 'game', after I had finished my chores, Mother slammed a plate of food in front of me. The cold leftovers were a feast to my eyes. But I was wary; it seemed too good to be true. 'Two minutes!' Mother barked. 'You have two minutes to eat. That's all.' Like lightning I picked up the fork, but the moment before the food touched my mouth, Mother snatched the plate away from me and emptied the food down the garbage disposal. 'Too late!' she sneered.

I stood before her dumbstruck. I didn't know what to do or say. All I could think of was '*Why?*' I couldn't understand why she treated me the way she did. I was so close that I could smell every morsel. I knew she wanted me to cave in, but I stood fast and held back the tears.

Alone in the garage, I felt I was losing control of everything. I craved food. I wanted my father. But more than anything, I wanted just an ounce of respect; one little bit of dignity. Sitting there on my hands, I could hear my brothers opening the refrigerator to get their desserts, and I hated it. I looked at myself. My skin had a yellowish tint, and my muscles were thin and stringy. Whenever I heard one of my brothers laugh at a television show, I cursed their names. '*Lucky bastards! Why doesn't she take turns and beat up on one of them for a change?*' I cried to myself as I vented my feelings of hatred.

For nearly ten days I had gone without food. I had just finished the dinner dishes when Mother repeated her 'you have two minutes to eat' game. There were only a few bits of food on the plate. I felt she would snatch the plate away again, so I moved with a purpose. I didn't give Mother a chance to snatch it away like she had the past three evenings. So I grabbed the plate and quickly swallowed the food without chewing it. Within seconds, I finished eating all that was on the plate and licked it clean. 'You eat like a pig!' Mother snarled. I bowed my head, acting as though I cared. But inside I laughed at her, saying to myself, *'Fuck you! Say what you want! I got the food!'*

Mother had another favorite game for me while Father was away. She sent me to clean the bathroom with her usual time limits. But this time, she put a bucket, filled with a mixture of ammonia and Clorox, in the room with me and closed the door. The first time she did this, Mother informed me she had read about it in a newspaper and wanted to try it. Even though I acted as if I were frightened, I really wasn't. I was ignorant about what was going to happen. Only when Mother closed the door and ordered me not to open it, did I begin to worry. With the room sealed, the air began to quickly change. In the corner of the bathroom I dropped to my hands and knees and stared at the bucket. A fine gray mist swirled towards the ceiling. As I breathed in the fumes, I collapsed and began spitting up. My throat felt like it was on fire. Within minutes it was raw. The gas from the reaction of the ammonia and Clorox mixture made my eyes water. I was frantic about not being able to meet Mother's time limits for cleaning the bathroom.

After a few more minutes, I thought I would cough up my insides. I knew that Mother wasn't going to give in and open the door. To survive her new game, I had to use my head. Laying on the tiled floor I stretched my body, and using my foot, I slide the bucket to the door. I did this for two reasons: I wanted the bucket as far away from me as possible, and in case Mother opened the door, I wanted her to get a snoot full of her own medicine. I curled up in the opposite corner of the bathroom, with my cleaning rag over my mouth, nose and eyes. Before covering my face, I wet the rag in the toilet. I didn't dare turn on the water in the sink for fear of Mother hearing it. Breathing through the cloth, I watched the mist inch its way closer and closer to the floor. I felt as if I were locked in a gas chamber. Then I thought about the small heating vent on the floor by my feet. I knew it turned on and off every few minutes. I put my face next to the vent and sucked in all the air my lungs would hold. In about half an hour, Mother opened the door and told me to empty the bucket into the drain in the garage before I smelled up *her* house. Downstairs I coughed up blood for over an hour. Of all Mother's punishments, I hated the gas chamber game the most.

Towards the end of summer Mother must have become bored with finding ways to torture me around the house. One day after I had completed all my morning chores, she sent me out to mow lawns. This wasn't an altogether new routine. During the Easter vacation from school the spring before, Mother had sent me out to mow. She had set a quota on my earnings and ordered me return the money to her. The quota was impossible for me to meet, so, in desperation, I once stole nine dollars from the piggy bank of a small girl who lived in our neighborhood. Within hours, the girl's father was knocking on the front door. Of course, Mother returned the money and blamed me. After the man left, she beat me until I was black and blue. I only stole the money to try to meet her quota.

The summer mowing plan turned out no better for me than the one during Easter vacation. Going from door to door, I asked people if they cared to have their lawns mowed. No one did. My ragged clothes and my thin arms must have made me a pathetic sight. Out of sympathy, one lady gave me a lunch in a brown bag and set me on my way. Half a block down the street a couple agreed to have me mow their lawn. When I finished, I started running back to Mother's house, carrying the brown bag with me. I intended to hide it before I turned onto her block. I didn't make it. Mother was out cruising in her car, and she pulled over and caught me with the bag. Before Mother screeched the station wagon to a stop, I threw my hands into the air, as if I were a criminal. I remember wishing that lady luck would be with me just one time.

Mother leaped out of the car, snatched the brown bag in one hand and punched me with the other. She then threw me into the car, and drove to the house where the lady had made the lunch for me. The woman wasn't home. Mother was convinced that I had sneaked into the lady's house and prepared my own lunch. I knew that to be in the possession of food was the ultimate crime. Silently, I yelled at myself for not ditching the food earlier.

Once home, the usual 'ten-rounder' left me sprawled on the floor. Mother then told me to sit outside in the backyard while she took 'her sons' to the zoo. The section where Mother ordered me to sit was covered with rocks about an inch in diameter. I lost circulation in much of my body, as I sat on my hands in my 'prisoner of war' position. I began to give up on God. I felt that He must have hated me. *What other reason could there be for a life like mine?* All my efforts for mere survival seemed futile. My attempts to stay one step ahead of Mother were useless. A black shadow was always over me.

Even the sun seemed to avoid me, as it hid in a thick cloud cover that drifted overhead. I slumped my shoulders, retreating into the solitude of my dreams. I don't know how much time had passed, but later I could hear the distinctive sound of Mother's station wagon returning into the garage. My time sitting on the rocks was over. I wondered what Mother had planned for me next. I prayed it was not another gas chamber session. She yelled from the garage for me to follow her upstairs. She led me to the bathroom. My heart sank. I felt doomed. I began taking huge breaths of fresh air, knowing that soon I would need it.

To my surprise there wasn't any bucket or bottles in the bathroom. '*Am I off the hook?*' I asked myself. This looked too easy. I timidly watched Mother as she turned the cold water tap in the bathtub fully open. I thought it was odd that she forgot to turn on the hot water as well. As the tub began to fill with cold water, Mother tore off my clothes and ordered me to get into the tub. I got into the tub and laid down. A cold fear raced throughout my body. 'Lower!' Mother yelled. 'Put your face in the water like this!' She then bent over, grabbed my neck with both hands and shoved my head under the water. Instinctively, I thrashed and kicked, trying desperately to force my head above the water so I could breathe. Her grip was too strong. Under the water I opened my eyes. I could see bubbles escape from my mouth and float to the surface as I tried to shout. I tried to thrust my head from side to side as I saw the bubbles becoming smaller and smaller. I began to feel weak. In a frantic effort I reached up and grabbed her shoulders. My fingers must have dug into her because Mother let go. She looked down on me, trying to get her breath. 'Now keep your head below the water, or next time it will be longer!'

I submerged my head, keeping my nostrils barely above the surface of the water. I felt like an alligator in a swamp. When Mother left the bathroom, her plan became more clear to me. As I laid stretched out in the tub, the water became unbearably cold. It was as though I was in a refrigerator. I was too frightened of Mother to move, so I kept my head under the surface as ordered.

Hours passed and my skin began to wrinkle. I didn't dare touch any part of my body to try to warm it. I did raise my head out of the water, far enough to hear better. Whenever I heard somebody walk down the hall outside the bathroom, I quietly slid my head back into the coldness.

Usually the footsteps I heard were one of my brothers going to their bedroom. Sometimes one of them came into the bathroom to use the toilet. They just glared at me, shook their heads and turned away. I tried to imagine I was in some other place, but I could not relax enough to daydream.

Before the family sat down for dinner, Mother came into the bathroom and yelled at me, telling me to get out of the bathtub and put on my clothes. I responded immediately, grabbing a towel to dry myself. 'Oh, no!' she screamed. 'Put your clothes on the way you are!' Without hesitating, I obeyed her command. My clothes were soaked as I ran downstairs to sit in the backyard as instructed. The sun had begun to set, but half the yard was still in direct sunlight. I tried to sit in a sunny area, but Mother ordered me into the shade. In the corner of the backyard, while sitting in my POW position, I shivered. I wanted only a few seconds of heat, but with every passing minute my chances of drying off were becoming less and less. From the upstairs window I could heard the sound of 'the family' passing dishes full of food to each other. Once in a while, a burst of laughter would escape through the window. Since Father was home, I knew that whatever Mother had cooked was good. I wanted to turn my head and look up to see them eating, but I didn't dare. I lived in a different world. I didn't even deserve a glance at the good life.

The bathtub and the backyard treatment soon became routine. At times when I laid in the tub, my brothers brought their friends to the bathroom to look at their naked brother. Their friends often scoffed at me. 'What did *he* do *this* time?' they'd ask. Most of the time my brothers just shook their heads, saying, 'I don't know.'

With the start of school in the fall, came the hope of

a temporary escape from my dreary life. Our fourth-grade homeroom class had a substitute teacher for the first two weeks. They told us that our regular teacher was ill. The substitute teacher was younger than most of the other staff, and she seemed more lenient. At the end of the first week, she passed out ice cream to those students whose behavior had been good. I didn't get any the first week, but I tried harder and received my reward at the end of the second week. The new teacher played 'pop hits' on 45-rpm records, and sang to the class. We really liked her. When Friday afternoon came, I didn't want to leave. After all the other students had gone, she bent close to me and told me I would have to go home. She knew I was a problem child. I told her that I wanted to stay with her. She held me for a moment, then got up and played the song I liked best. After that I left. Since I was late, I ran to the house as fast as I could and raced through my chores. When I was finished, Mother sent me to the backyard to sit on the cold cement deck.

That Friday, I looked up at the thick blanket of fog covering the sun, and cried inside. The substitute teacher had been so nice to me. She treated me like a real person, not like some piece of filth lying in the gutter. As I sat outside feeling sorry for myself, I wondered where she was and what she was doing. I didn't understand it at the time, but I had a crush on her.

I knew that I wasn't going to be fed that night, or the next. Since Father wasn't home, I would have a bad weekend. Sitting in the cool air in the backyard, on the steps, I could hear the sounds of Mother feeding my brothers. I didn't care. Closing my eyes, I could see the smiling face of my new teacher. That night as I sat outside shivering, her beauty and kindness kept me warm.

By October, my morbid life was in full swing. Food was scarce at school. I was easy prey for school bullies, who beat me up at will. After school I had to run to the house and spill the contents of my stomach for Mother's inspection. Sometimes she would have me start my chores right away. Sometimes she would fill the bathtub with water. If she was *really* in a good mood, she fixed up the gas mixture for me in the bathroom. If she got tired of having me around her house, she sent me out to find some mowing jobs, but not before beating me. A few times she whipped me with the dog's chain. It was very painful, but I just gritted my teeth and took it. The worst pain was a blow to the backs of my legs with the broom handle. Sometimes blows from the broom handle would leave me on the floor, barely able to move. More than once I hobbled down the street, pushing that old wooden lawn mower, trying to earn *her* some money.

There finally came a time when it didn't do me any good for Father to be home because Mother had forbidden him to see me. My hope deteriorated and I began to believe that my life would never change. I thought I would be Mother's slave for as long as I lived. With every passing day, my willpower became weaker. I no longer dreamed of Superman or some imaginary hero who would come and rescue me. I knew that Father's promise to take me away was a hoax. I gave up praying and thought only of living my life one day at a time.

One morning at school, I was told to report to the school nurse. She questioned me about my clothes and the various bruises that spanned the length of both my arms. At first I told her what Mother had instructed me to tell her. But as my trust in her began to grow, I told her more and more about Mother. She took notes and told me I should come to see her anytime I wanted to talk to somebody. I learned later that the nurse became interested in me because of some reports she had received from the substitute teacher, earlier in the school year.

During the last week in October, it was tradition at Mother's house for the boys to carve designs on pumpkins. I had been denied this privilege since I was seven or eight years old. When the night came to carve the pumpkins, Mother filled the tub just as soon as I had finished my chores. Again she warned me about keeping my head under the water. As a reminder, she grabbed my neck and pushed my head under the water. Then she stormed out of the bathroom, turning the light out as she went. Looking to my left, I could see through the small bathroom window that night was beginning to fall. I passed the time by counting to myself. I started at one and stopped at one thousand. Then I started over. As the hours passed, I could feel the water slowly draining away. As the water drained, my body became colder and colder. I cupped my hands between my legs and laid the length of my body against the right side of the bathtub. I could hear the sounds of Stan's Halloween record that Mother had bought for him several years before. Ghosts and ghouls howled, and doors creaked open. After the boys had carved their pumpkins, I could hear Mother in her soothing voice telling them a scary story. The more I heard, the more I hated each and every one of them. It was bad enough waiting like a dog out in the backyard on the rocks while they enjoyed dinner, but having to lay in the cold bathtub, shivering to keep warm while they ate popcorn and listened to Mother's tales made me want to scream.

Mother's tone of voice that night reminded me of the kind of Mommy I had loved so many years ago. Now, even the boys refused to acknowledge my presence in the house. I meant less to them than the spirits that howled from Stan's record. After the boys went to bed, Mother came into the bathroom. She appeared startled to see me still laying in the bathtub. 'Are you cold?' she sneered. I shivered and shook my head indicating that I was very cold. 'Well, why doesn't my precious little boy get his ass out of the bathtub and warm his hide in his father's bed?'

I stumbled out of the tub, put on my underwear and crawled into Father's bed, soaking the sheets with my wet body. For reasons I didn't understand Mother had decided to have me sleep in the master bedroom, whether Father was home or not. She slept in the upstairs bedroom with my brothers. I didn't really care as long as I didn't have to sleep on the army cot in the cold garage. That night Father came home, but before I could say anything to him, I fell asleep.

By Christmas, my spirit was drained. I detested being home during the two-week vacation and impatiently awaited my return to school. On Christmas Day I received a pair of roller skates. I was surprised to get anything at all, but as it turned out, the skates were not a gift given in the spirit of Christmas. The skates proved to be just another tool for Mother to get me out of the house and make me suffer. On weekends Mother made me skate outside when the other children were inside because of the chilly weather. I skated up and down the block, without even a jacket to keep me warm. I was the only child outside in the neighborhood. More than once, Tony, one of our neighbors, stepped outside to get his afternoon newspaper and saw me skating. He'd give me a cheerful smile before scurrying back inside to get away from the cold. In an effort to keep warm, I skated as fast as I could. I could see smoke rising from the chimneys of houses that had fireplaces. I wished that I could be inside, sitting by a fire. Mother had me skate for hours at a time. She called me in, only when she wanted me to complete some chores for her.

At the end of March that year, Mother went into labor while we were home from school on Easter vacation. As Father drove her to a hospital in San Francisco, I prayed that it was the real thing and not false labor. I wanted Mother out of the house so badly. I knew that with her gone, Father would feed me. I was also happy to be free from the beatings.

While Mother was in the hospital, Father let me play with my brothers. I was immediately accepted back into the fold. We played 'Star Trek', and Ron gave me the honor of playing the role of Captain Kirk. The first day Father served sandwiches for lunch and let me have seconds. When Father went to the hospital to see Mother, the four of us played across the street at the home of a neighbor named Shirley. Shirley was kind to us and treated us as though we were her own children. She kept us entertained with games like ping-pong, or just let us run wild outside. In some ways Shirley reminded me of Mom, in the early days before she started beating me.

In a few days, Mother came home. She presented

the family with a new baby brother named Kevin. After a few weeks had passed, things returned to normal. Father stayed away most of the time, and I continued to be the scapegoat upon which Mother vented her frustrations.

Mother rarely spent much time with neighbors, so it was not natural for her when she and Shirley became close friends. They visited each other daily. In Shirley's presence Mother played the role of the loving, caring parent – just as she had when she was a Cub Scout den mother. After several months, Shirley asked Mother why David was not allowed to play with the other children. She was also curious why David was punished so often. Mother had a variety of excuses. David either had a cold or he was working on a school project. Eventually, she told Shirley that David was a bad boy and deserved being grounded for a long, long time.

In time, the relationship between Shirley and Mother became strained. One day, for no apparent reason, Mother broke all ties with Shirley. Shirley's son was not allowed to play with the boys, and mother ran around the house calling her a bitch. Even though

I wasn't allowed to play with the others, I felt a little safer when Shirley and Mother were friends.

One Sunday during the last month of summer, Mother came into the master bedroom where I had been ordered to sit on my hands in my POW position. She asked me to get up and sit on the corner of the bed. She then told me that she was tired of the life we were living. She told me she was sorry and that she wanted to make up for all the lost time. I smiled from ear to ear, as I jumped into her arms and held her tightly. As she ran her hand through my hair, I began to cry. Mother cried too, and I began to feel that my bad times were finished. I let go of our hug and looked into Mother's eyes. I had to know for sure. I had to hear her say it again. 'Is it really over?' I asked timidly.

'It's over, sweetheart. After this moment, I want you to forget any of it happened at all. You will try to be a good boy, won't you?'

I shook my head.

'Then, I'll try to be a good mother.'

After making up, Mom let me take a warm bath and put on the new clothes I had received last Christmas. I had not been allowed to wear them before. Mom then took my brothers and I bowling while Father stayed home with Kevin. On the way home from the bowling alley, Mom stopped at a grocery store and bought each of us a toy top. When we got home, Mom said I could play outside with the other boys, but I took the top to the corner of the master bedroom and played by myself. For the first time in years, with the exception of holidays when we had guests in the house, I ate with my family at the dinner table. Things were happening too fast, and I felt that somehow it was too good to be true. As happy as I was, I felt as though I were walking on eggshells. I thought for sure Mother would wake up and change back to her old self. But she didn't. I ate all I wanted for dinner, and she let me watch television with my brothers before we went to bed. I thought it was strange that she wanted me to continue to sleep with Father, but she said she wanted to be near the baby.

The next day, while Father was at work, a lady from social services came to our house in the afternoon. Mom shooed me outside to play with my brothers, while she talked to the lady. They talked for more than an hour. Before the lady left, Mom called me into our house. The lady wanted to talk to me for a few minutes. She wanted to know if I was happy. I told her

I was. She wanted to know if I got along all right with my mom. I told her I did. Finally, she asked me if Mom ever beat me. Before answering, I looked up at Mother, who smiled politely. I felt as though a bomb had exploded deep in the pit of my stomach. I thought I would throw up. It had suddenly occurred to me why Mother had changed the day before; why she had been so nice to me. I felt like a fool because I had fallen for it. I was so hungry for love that I had swallowed the whole charade.

Mother's hand on my shoulder brought me back to reality. 'Well, tell her, sweetheart,' Mother said, smiling again. 'Tell her that I starve you and beat you like a dog,' Mother snickered, trying to get the lady to laugh too.

I looked at the lady. My face felt flushed, and I could feel the beads of sweat forming on my forehead. I didn't have the guts to tell the lady the truth. 'No, it's not like that at all,' I said. 'Mom treats me pretty good.'

'And she never beats you?' the lady asked.

'No . . . uh . . . I mean, only when I get punished . . . when I'm a bad boy,' I said, trying to cover up the truth. I could tell by the look Mother gave me that I

125

had said the wrong thing. She had brainwashed me for years, and I had said it badly. I could also tell that the lady had picked up on the communication between Mother and I.

'All right,' the lady said. 'I just wanted to stop in and say hello.' After saying goodbye, Mother walked her visitor to the door.

When the lady was clearly gone, Mother closed the door in a rage. 'You little shit!' she screamed. I instinctively covered my face as she began swinging. She hit me several times, then banished me to the garage. After she had fed her boys, she called me up to do my evening chores. As I washed the dishes, I didn't feel all that bad. Deep in my heart I had known Mother was being nice to me for some reason other than wanting to love me. I should have known she didn't mean it, because she acted the same way when somebody like Grandma came over for the holidays. At least I had enjoyed two good days. I hadn't had two good days for a long time, so in an odd way it was worth it. I settled back into my routine and relied on my solitude to keep me going. At least I didn't have to walk on eggshells anymore, wondering when the roof was going to cave in on me. Things were back to normal, and I was the servant for the family again.

Even though I had begun to accept my fate, I never felt as alone, as I did on the mornings that Father went to work. He got out of bed about 5:00 A.M. on work days. He didn't know it, but I was always awake too. I'd listen to him shaving in the bathroom, and I would hear him walking to the kitchen to get something to eat. I knew that when he put on his shoes, he was about ready to leave the house. Sometimes I turned over just in time to see him pick up his dark blue, Pam Am overnight bag. He'd kiss me on the forehead and say, 'Try to make her happy and stay out of her way.'

I tried not to cry, but I always did. I didn't want him to leave. I never told him, but I am sure he knew. After he closed the front door, I counted the steps that it took him to get to the driveway. I heard him walking on the pathway from the house. In my mind, I could see him turning left down the block to catch the bus to San Francisco. Sometimes, when I felt brave, I hopped out of bed and ran to the window so I could catch a glimpse of Father. I usually stayed in bed and rolled over to the warm place where he had slept. I imagined that I could hear him long after he was gone.

And when I accepted the fact that he was truly gone, I had a cold, hollow feeling deep in my soul. I loved my Father so much. I wanted to be with him forever, and I cried inside because I never knew when I was going to see Father again.

Chapter 7
# The Lord's Prayer

About a month before I entered the fifth grade, I came to believe that for me, there was no God.

As I sat alone in the garage, or read to myself in the near darkness of my parents' bedroom, I came to realize that I would live like this for the remainder of my life. No *just* God would leave me like this. I believed that I was alone in my struggle and that my battle was one of survival.

By the time I had decided that there was no God, I had totally disconnected myself from all physical pain. Whenever Mother struck me, it was as if she were taking her aggressions out on a rag doll. Inside, my emotions swirled back and forth between fear and intense anger. But outside, I was a robot, rarely revealing my emotions; only when I thought it would please The Bitch and work to my advantage. I held in my tears, refusing to cry because I didn't want to give *her* the satisfaction of my defeat.

At night I no longer dreamed, nor did I let my imagination work during the day. The once vibrant escapes of watching myself fly through the clouds in bright blue costumes, were now a thing of the past. When I fell asleep, my soul became consumed in a black void. I no longer awoke in the mornings refreshed; I was tired and told myself that I had one day less to live in this world. I shuffled through my chores, dreading every moment of every day. With no dreams, I found that words like *hope* and *faith* were only letters, randomly put together into something meaningless – words only for fairy tales.

When I *was* given the luxury of food, I ate like a homeless dog; grunting like an animal at Mother's commands. I no longer cared when she made fun of me, as I hurried to devour even the smallest morsel. Nothing was beneath me. One Saturday while I was washing the morning dishes, Mother scraped some half-eaten pancakes from a plate, into the dogs' dish. Her well-fed pets picked at the food until they wanted no more, then walked away to find a place to sleep. Later, as I put away some pots and pans in a lower cabinet, I crawled on my hands and knees to the dogs' dish and ate what was left of the pancakes. As I ate, I could smell traces of the dogs, but I ate anyway. It hardly bothered me. I fully realized that if The Bitch caught me eating what rightfully belonged to the dogs, I would pay dearly; but getting food any way I could was my only means of existing.

Inside, my soul became so cold I hated everything. I even despised the sun, for I knew I would never be able to play in its warm presence. I cringed with hate whenever I heard other children laughing, as they played outside. My stomach coiled whenever I smelled food that was about to be served to somebody else, knowing it was not for me. I wanted so much to strike out at something every time I was called upstairs to play the role of the family slave, by picking up after those slobs.

I hated Mother most and wished that she were dead. But before she died, I wanted her to feel the magnitude of my pain and my loneliness for all these years. During all the years when I had prayed to God, He answered me only once. One day, when I was five or six years old, Mother had thrashed me from one end of the house to the other. That night before getting into bed, I got down on my knees and prayed to God. I asked Him to make Mother sick so she couldn't hit me any more. I prayed long and hard, concentrating so much that I went to bed with a headache. The next morning, much to my surprise, Mother was sick. She lay on the couch all day, barely moving. Since Father was at work, my brothers and I took care of her as though she were a patient of ours.

As the years passed and the beatings became more intense, I thought about Mother's age and tried to calculate when she might die. I longed for the day when *her* soul would be taken into the depths of hell; only then would I be free of her.

I also hated Father. He was fully aware of the hell I lived in, but he lacked the courage to rescue me as he had promised so many times in the past. But as I examined my relationship with Father, I realized that he considered me part of the problem. I believe he thought of me as a traitor. Many times when The Bitch and Father had heated arguments, Mother involved me. She would yank me from wherever I was and demand that I repeat every vile word Father might have used in their past arguments. I fully realized what her game was, but having to choose between them was not difficult. Mother's wrath was much worse for me. I always shook my head, timidly saying what she wanted to hear. She would then scream for me to repeat the words to her in Dad's presence. Much of the time she insisted that I make up the words if I couldn't remember. This bothered me a great deal because I knew that in an effort to avoid a beating, I was biting the hand that often fed me. In the beginning, I tried to explain to Father why I had lied and turned against him. At first he told me that he understood, but eventually I knew he had lost faith in me. Instead of feeling sorry for him, I only hated him more.

The boys who lived upstairs were no longer my brothers. Sometimes in years past, they had managed to encourage me a little. But in the summer of 1972 they took turns hitting me and appeared to enjoy throwing their weight around. It was obvious that they felt superior to the family slave. When they approached me, my heart became hard as stone, and I am sure they saw the hate etched in my face. In a rare and empty victory, I'd sneer the word '*asshole*' under my breath as one of them strutted by me. I made sure they didn't hear me. I came to despise the neighbors, my relatives and anybody else who had ever known me and the conditions under which I lived. Hate was all I had left.

At the core of my soul, I hated myself more than anybody or anything. I came to believe that everything that happened to me or around me was my own fault because I had let it go on for so long. I wanted what others had, but saw no way to get it, so I hated them for having it. I wanted to be strong, but inside I knew I was a wimp. I never had the courage to stand up to The Bitch, so I knew I deserved whatever happened to me. For years, Mother had brainwashed me by having me shout aloud, 'I hate myself! I hate myself!' Her efforts paid off. A few weeks before I started the fifth grade, I hated myself so much that I wished I were dead.

School no longer held the exciting appeal that it had years ago. I struggled to concentrate on my work while in class, but my bottled-up anger often flashed at the wrong times. One Friday afternoon in the winter of 1973, for no apparent reason, I stormed out of the classroom, screaming at everyone as I fled. I slammed the door so hard I thought the glass above the door would shatter. I ran to the bathroom, and with my tiny red fist I pounded the tiles until my strength drained away. Afterwards, I collapsed on the floor praying for a miracle. It never came.

Time spent outside the classroom was only better than Mother's 'hell house'. Because I was an outcast of the entire school, my classmates at times took over where Mother left off. One of them was Clifford, a school-yard bully who would periodically catch me when I ran to Mother's house after school. Beating me up was Clifford's way of showing off to his friends. All I could do was fall to the ground and cover my head, while Clifford and his gang took turns kicking me.

Aggie was a tormentor of a different sort. She never failed to come up with new and different ways of telling me how much she wished I would simply 'drop dead'. Her style was absolute snobbery. Aggie made sure she was always the one in charge of a small band of girls. In addition to tormenting me, showing off their fancy clothes seemed to be the main purpose in life for Aggie and her clique. I had always known Aggie didn't like me, but I really didn't learn how much until the last day of school in our fourth-grade year. Aggie's mother taught my fourth-grade homeroom, and on the last day of school Aggie came into our room acting as though she were throwing up and said, 'David Pelzer-Smellzer is going to be in my home-room next year.' Her day was not complete until she fired off a rude remark about me to her friends.

I didn't take Aggie very seriously; not until a fifth-grade field trip to one of San Francisco's Clipper Ships. As I stood alone on the bow of the ship, looking at the water, Aggie approached me with a vicious smile and said in a low voice, 'Jump!' She startled me, and I looked into her face, trying to understand what she meant. Again she spoke, quietly and calmly, 'I said you should go ahead and jump. I know all about you Pelzer, and jumping is your only way out.'

Another voice came from behind her, 'She's right, you know.' The voice belonged to John, another classmate, one of Aggie's macho buddies. Looking back over the railing, I stared at the cold, green water lapping against the wooden side of the ship. For a moment, I could visualize myself plunging into the water, knowing I would drown. It was a comforting thought that promised an escape from Aggie, her friends and all that I hated in the world. But my better senses returned, and I looked up and fixed my eyes directly on John's eyes and tried to hold my stare.

After a few moments, he must have felt my anger because he turned away taking Aggie with him.

At the beginning of my fifth-grade year, Mr Ziegler, my homeroom teacher, had no idea why I was such a problem child. Later, after the school nurse had informed him why I had stolen food and why I dressed the way I did, Mr Ziegler made a special effort to treat me as if I were a normal kid. One of his jobs as sponsor of the school newspaper was to form a committee of kids to find a name for the paper. I came up with a catchy phrase, and a week later my entry was among others in a school-wide election to select the best name for the newspaper. My title won by a landslide. Later that day the voting took place, and Mr Ziegler took me aside and told me how proud he was that my title had won. I soaked it up like a sponge. I hadn't been told anything positive for so long that I nearly cried. At the end of the day, after assuring me that I wasn't in trouble, Mr Ziegler gave me a letter to take to Mother.

Elated, I ran to Mother's house faster than ever before. As I should have expected, my happiness was short-lived. The Bitch tore the letter open, read it quickly and scoffed, 'Well, Mr Ziegler says I should be so proud of you for naming the school newspaper. He also claims that you are one of the top pupils in his class. Well, aren't you special?' Suddenly, her voice turned ice cold and she jabbed her finger at my face and hissed, 'Get one thing straight, you little son of a bitch! There is nothing you can do to impress me! Do you understand me? You are a *nobody*! An *It*! You are nonexistent! You are a bastard child! I hate you and I wish you were dead! *Dead!* Do you hear me? *Dead!*'

After tearing the letter into tiny pieces, Mother turned away from me and returned to her television show. I stood motionless, gazing at the letter which lay like snowflakes at my feet. Even though I had heard the same words over and over again, this time the word '*It*' stunned me like never before. She had stripped me of my very existence. I gave all that I could to accomplish anything positive for *her* recognition. But again, I failed. My heart sank lower than ever before. Mother's words were no longer coming from the booze; they were coming from her heart. I would have been relieved if she had returned with a knife and ended it all.

I knelt down, trying to put the many pieces of the letter back together again. It was impossible. I dumped the pieces of the letter in the trash, wishing my life would end. I truly believed, at that moment, that death would be better than my prospects for any kind of happiness. I was nothing but an '*It*'.

My morale had become so low that in some self-destructive way I hoped she would kill me, and I felt that eventually she would. In my mind it was just a matter of when she would do it. So I began to purposefully irritate her, hoping I could provoke her enough that she would end my misery. I began doing my chores in a careless manner. I made sure that I forgot to wipe the bathroom floor, hoping that Mother or one of her royal subjects might slip and fall, hurting themselves on the hard tile floor. When I washed the evening dishes, I left bits of food on the plates. I wanted The Bitch to know I didn't care anymore.

As my attitude began to change, I became more and more rebellious. A crisis erupted one day at the grocery store. Usually I stayed in the car, but for some reason Mother decided to take me inside. She ordered me to keep one hand clamped onto the cart and bend my head towards the floor. I deliberately disobeyed her every command. I knew she didn't want to make a scene in public, so I walked in front of the cart, making sure I was at least an arm's length away from her. If my brothers made any comments to me, I fired back at them. I simply told myself that I wasn't going to take anybody's crap anymore.

Mother knew that the other shoppers were watching us and could hear us, so several times she gently took my arm and told me in a pleasant voice to settle down. I felt so alive knowing I had the upper hand in the store, but I also knew that once we were outside, I would pay the price. Just as I thought, Mother gave me a sound thrashing before we reached the station wagon. As soon as we were in the car, she ordered me to lie on the floor of the back seat, where her boys took turns stomping me with their feet for 'mouthing off' to them and Mother. Immediately after we entered the house, Mother made a special batch of ammonia and Clorox. She must have guessed I had been using the rag as a mask because she tossed the rag into the bucket. As soon as she slammed the bathroom door, I hurried to the heating vent. It didn't come on. No fresh air came through the vent. I must have been in the bathroom for over an hour because the gray fumes filled the small room all the way to the floor. My eyes filled with tears, which seemed to activate the poison even more. I spat mucus and heaved until I thought I would faint. When Mother finally opened the door, I bolted for the hallway, but her hand seized me by the neck. She tried to push my face into the bucket, but I fought back and she failed. After the longer 'gas chamber' incident, I returned to my wimpy self, but deep inside I could still feel the pressure building like a volcano, waiting to erupt from deep inside my soul.

The only thing that kept me sane was my baby brother Kevin. He was a beautiful baby and I loved him. About three and a half months before he was born, Mother allowed me to watch a Christmas cartoon special. After the program, for reasons unclear to me, she ordered me to sit in my brothers room. Minutes later she stormed into the room, wrapped her hands around my neck and began choking me. I twisted my head from side to side, trying to squirm away from her grip. As I began to feel faint, I instinctively kicked her legs, forcing her away from me. I soon regretted the incident.

About a month after Mother's attempt to choke me, she told me that I had kicked her so hard in the stomach that the baby would have a permanent birth defect. I felt like a murderer. Mother didn't stop with just telling me. She had several different versions of the incident for anybody who would listen. She said she had tried to hug me, and I had repeatedly either kicked or punched her in the stomach. She claimed that I had kicked her because I was jealous of the new baby. She said I was afraid the new baby would get more of her attention. I really loved Kevin, but since I was not allowed to even *look* at him or my brothers, I did not have a chance to show how I felt. I do remember one Saturday, when Mother took the other boys to a baseball game in Oakland, leaving Father to babysit with Kevin while I performed my chores. After I finished my work, Father let Kevin out of his crib. I enjoyed watching him crawl around in his cute outfit. I thought he was beautiful. When Kevin lifted his head and smiled at me, my heart melted. He made me forget my suffering for awhile. His innocence was hypnotic as I followed him around the house; I wiped the drool from his mouth and stayed one step behind him so he wouldn't get hurt. Before Mother returned, I played a game of patty-cake with him. The sound of Kevin's laughter filled my heart with warmth, and later, whenever I felt depressed I thought of him. I smiled inside when I heard Kevin cry out in joy.

My brief encounter with Kevin quickly faded away and my hatred surfaced again. I fought to bury my feelings, but I couldn't. I knew I was never meant to be loved. I knew I would never live a life like my brothers. Worst of all, I knew that it was only a matter of time until Kevin would hate me, just like the others did.

Later that fall, Mother began directing her frustrations in more directions. She despised me as much as ever, but she began to alienate her friends, husband, brother and even her own mother. Even as a small child, I knew that Mother didn't get along very well with her family. She felt that everybody was trying to tell her what to do. She never felt at ease, especially with her own mother who was also a strong-willed person. Grandmother usually offered to buy Mother a new dress or take her to the beauty parlor. Not only did Mother refuse the offers, but she also yelled and screamed until Grandmother left *her* house. Sometimes Grandmother tried to help me, but that only made things worse. Mother insisted that her appearance and the way she raised her family were 'nobody else's damn business.' After a few of these confrontations, Grandmother rarely visited Mother's house.

As the holiday season approached, Mother argued more and more with Grandmother on the telephone. She called her own mother every vicious name Mother could imagine. The trouble between Mother and Grandmother was bad for me because after their battle, I often became the object of Mother's anger. Once, from the basement, I heard Mother call my brothers into the kitchen and tell them that they no longer had a Grandmother or an Uncle Dan.

Mother was equally ruthless in her relationship with Father. When he did come home, either to visit or stay for a day, she started screaming at him the moment he walked through the door. As a result, he often came home drunk. In an effort to stay out of Mother's path, Father often spent his time doing odd jobs outside the house. He even caught her wrath at work. She often telephoned Father at the station and called him names. 'Worthless' and 'drunken loser' were two of her favorite names for him. After a few calls, the fireman who answered the phone would lay it down and not page Father. This made Mother furious, and again I became the object of her fury.

For awhile Mother banned Father from the house, and the only time we saw him was when we drove to San Francisco to pick up his pay-check. One time, on our way to get the check, we drove through Golden Gate Park. Even though my anger was ever present, I flashed back to the good times when the park meant so much to the whole family. My brothers were also silent that day as we drove through the park. Everybody seemed to sense that somehow the park had lost its glamour, and that things would never be the same again. I think that perhaps my brothers felt the good times were over for them too.

For a short time Mother's attitude towards Father changed. One Sunday, Mother piled everybody into the car, and shopped from store to store for a record of German songs. She wanted to create a special mood for Father when he came home. She spent most of that afternoon preparing a feast, with the same enthusiasm that had driven her years before. It took her hours to fix her hair and apply her makeup just right. Mother even put on a dress that brought back memories of the person she once was. I thought for sure that God had answered my prayers. As she paced around the house, straightening anything she thought was out of place, all I could think about was the food. I knew she would find it in her heart to let me eat with the family. It was an empty hope.

Time dragged on into the late afternoon. Father was expected to be home by about 1:00 P.M., and every time Mother heard an approaching car she dashed to the front door, waiting to greet him with open arms. Sometime after 4:00 P.M., Father came staggering in with a friend from work. The festive mood and setting were a surprise to him. From the bedroom I could hear Mother's strained voice as she tried to be extra patient with Father. A few minutes later, Father stumbled into the bedroom. I looked up in wonder. I had never seen him so drunk. He didn't need to speak for me to smell the liquor on him. His eyes were beyond the bloodshot stage, and it appeared to be more of a problem than he could manage to stand upright and keep his eyes open. Even before he opened the closet door, I knew what was he was going to do. I knew why he had come home. As he stuffed his blue overnight bag, I began to cry inside. I wanted to become small enough to jump into his bag and go with him.

When he finished packing, Father knelt down and

mumbled something to me. The longer I looked at him, the weaker my legs felt. My mind was numb with questions. *Where's my Hero? What happened to him?* As he opened the door to leave the bedroom, the drunk friend crashed into Father, nearly knocking him down. Father shook his head and said in a sad voice, 'I can't take it anymore. The whole thing. Your mother, this house, you. I just can't take it anymore.' Before he closed the bedroom door I could barely hear him mutter, 'I . . . I'm . . . I'm sorry.'

That year Thanksgiving dinner was a flop. In some kind of gesture of good faith, Mother allowed me to eat at the table with the family. I sat deep in my chair, quietly concentrating so I wouldn't say or do anything that might set Mother off. I could feel the tension between my parents. They hardly spoke at all, and my brothers chewed their food in silence. Dinner was hardly over when harsh words erupted. After the fight ended, Father left. Mother reached into one of the cabinets for her bottled prize and seated herself at the end of the sofa. She sat alone, pouring glass after glass of alcohol. As I cleared the table and washed the dishes, I could see that this time I wasn't the only one affected by Mother's behavior. My brothers seemed to be experiencing the same fear I had for so many years.

For a short time, Mother and Father tried to be civil to one another. But by Christmas Day, they had both become tired of their charade. The strain of trying to be so nice to each other was more than either could bear. As I sat at the top of the stairs, while my brothers finished opening their gifts, I could hear angry words being exchanged between them. I prayed that they could somehow make up, if only for that special day. While sitting on the basement stairs that Christmas morning, I knew that if God had wanted Mother and Father to be happy, then I would have to be dead.

A few days later, Mother packed Father's clothes in boxes, and drove with my brothers and I to a place a few blocks from the fire station. There, in front of a dingy motel, Father waited. His face seemed to express relief. My heart sank. After years of my useless prayers, I knew it had finally happened – my parents were separating. I closed my fists so tightly I thought my fingers would tear into the palms of my hands. While Mother and the boys went into Father's motel room, I sat in the car, cursing his name over and over. I hated him so much for running out on his family. But perhaps even more, I was jealous of him, for he had escaped and I had not. I still had to live with Mother. Before Mother drove the car away, Father leaned down to the open window where I was sitting, and handed me a package. It was some information he had said he would get me, for a book report that I was doing at school. I knew he was relieved to get away from Mother, but I could also see sadness in his eyes as we pulled away into the downtown traffic.

The drive back to Daly city was solemn. When my brothers spoke, they did so in soft tones that wouldn't upset Mother. When we reached the city limits, Mother tried to humor her boys by treating them to McDonald's. As usual, I sat in the car while they went inside. I looked out the open car window at the sky. A dull gray blanket covered everything, and I could feel the cold droplets of fog on my face. As I stared into the fog, I became terrified. I knew nothing could stop Mother now. What little hope I had was gone. I no longer had the will to carry on. I felt as if I were a man on death row, not knowing when my time would come.

I wanted to bolt from the car, but I was too scared to even move an inch. For this weakness, I hated myself. Rather than running, I clutched the package Father had given me and smelled it, trying to pick up a scent of Father's cologne.

When I failed to pick up any odor at all, I let out a sobbing cry. At that instant, I hated God more than anything else in this or any other world. God had known of my struggles for years, but He had stood by watching as things went from bad to worse. He wouldn't even grant me a trace of Father's Old Spice After Shave. God had completely taken away my greatest hope. Inside I cursed His name, wishing I had never been born.

Outside, I could hear the sounds of Mother and the boys approaching the car. I quickly wiped my tears and returned to the inner safety of my hardened shell. As Mother drove out of the McDonald's parking lot, she glanced back at me and sneered, 'You are all mine now. Too bad your father's not here to protect you.' I knew all my defenses were useless. I wasn't going to survive. I knew she was going to kill me, if not today, tomorrow. That day I wished Mother would have mercy and kill me quickly.

As my brothers wolfed down their hamburgers, without them knowing I clasped my hands together, bent my head down, closed my eyes and prayed with all my heart. When the station wagon turned onto the driveway, I felt that my time had come. Before I opened the car door, I bowed my head and with a peace in my heart, I whispered, '. . . and deliver me from evil.'

'Amen.'

# Sonoma County, California

*I'm so alive.*

*As I stand facing the beauty of the never-ending Pacific Ocean, a late afternoon breeze blows down from the hills behind. As always, it is a beautiful day. The sun is making its final descent. The magic is about to begin. The skies are ready to burn with brilliance, as it turns from a soft blue to a bright orange. Looking towards the West, I stare in awe at the hypnotic power of the waves. A giant curl begins to take form, then breaks with a thundering clap as it crashes on the shore. An invisible mist hits my face, moments before the white foamy water nearly drowns my feet. The bubbling foam quickly recedes to the power of the surf. Suddenly, a piece of driftwood washes onto the shore. It has an odd, twisted shape. The wood is pitted, yet smoothed and bleached from its time in the sun. I bend down to pick it up. As my fingers begin to reach out, the water catches hold dragging the wood back out to sea. For a moment, it looks as if the wood is struggling to stay ashore. It leaves a trail behind before reaching the waters, where it bobs violently before giving in to the ocean.*

*I marvel at the wood, thinking how it reminds me of my former life. My beginning was extremely turbulent, being pushed and pulled in every direction. The more grisly my situation became, the more I felt as if some immense power were sucking me into some giant undertow. I fought as hard as I could, but the cycle never seemed to end. Until suddenly, without warning, I broke free.*

*I'm so lucky. My dark past is behind me now. As bad as it was, I knew even back then, in the final analysis, my way of life would be up to me. I made a promise to myself that if I came out of my situation alive, I had to make something of myself. I would be the best person that I could be. Today I am. I made sure I let go of my past, accepting the fact that that part of my life was only a small fraction of my life. I knew the black hole was out there, waiting to suck me in and forever control my destiny – but only if I let it. I took positive control over my life.*

## Epilogue: Sonoma County, California

*I'm so blessed. The challenges of my past have made me immensely strong inside. I adapted quickly, learning how to survive from a bad situation. I learned the secret of internal motivation. My experience gave me a different outlook on life, that others may never know. I have a vast appreciation for things that others may take for granted. Along the way I made a few mistakes, but I was fortunate enough to bounce back. Instead of dwelling on the past, I maintained the same focus that I had taught myself years ago in the garage, knowing the good Lord was always over my shoulder, giving me quiet encouragement and strength when I needed it most.*

*My blessings also mean having the opportunity to meet so many people who had a positive impact on my life. The endless sea of faces, prodding me, teaching me to make the right choices, and helping me in my quest for success. They encouraged my hunger to prevail. Branching out on a different level, I enlisted in the United States Air Force, discovering historical values and an instilled sense of pride and belonging that until then, I had never known. After years of struggle, my purpose became clear; for above all, I came to realize that America was truly the land where one could come from less than humble beginnings, to become a winner from within.*

*An explosive pounding of the surf brings me back to reality. The piece of wood I've been watching, disappears into the swirling waters. Without further hesitation, I quickly turn away and head back towards my truck. Moments later, I race my Toyota through the snake-like turns driving to my secret utopia. Years ago when I lived in the dark, I used to dream about my secret place. Now, whenever I can get away, I always return to the river. After stopping to pick up my precious cargo at the Rio Villa in nearby Monte Rio, I'm back on the single-lane black top. For me, it is a race against time, for the sun is about to set and one of my lifetime dreams is about to come true.*

*As I enter the serene city of Guerneville, the 4-Runner truck goes from a Mach-like speed to that of a snail. I tap on the brakes before turning right, onto Riverside drive. With the windows rolled down, I fill my lungs full of sweet, purified air from the towering redwoods that gently sway back and forth.*

*I bring the white Toyota to a stop, in front of the same home where a lifetime ago my family and I stayed during our summer vacations. 17426 Riverside Drive. Like many things, the house, too, has changed. Years ago, two tiny bedrooms were added behind the fireplace.*

## Epilogue: Sonoma County, California

A vague attempt of expanding the tiny kitchen was made before the flood of 1986. Even the mighty tree stump, which, years ago, my brothers and I spent endless hours climbing, is now in decay. Only the cabin's darkened cedar ceiling and the river-stone fireplace have been left unchanged.

I feel a little sad as I turn away, strolling across the small gravel road. Then, making sure not to disturb anyone, I lead my son, Stephen, through a tiny passage beside the same house that my parents led my brothers and I through, years ago. I know the owner and I am sure he wouldn't mind. Without saying a word, my son and I gaze westward. The Russian River is the same as it always was, dark green and as smooth as glass, as it flows ever so gently to the mighty Pacific. Bluejays call to each other as they glide through the air, before disappearing into the redwoods. The sky above is now bathed with streaks of orange and blue. I take another deep breath and close my eyes, savoring the moment like I did years ago.

As I open my eyes, a single tear rolls down the side of my cheek. I kneel down wrapping my arms around Stephen's shoulders. Without hesitation, he leans his head back and gives me a kiss. 'Love you, Dad.'

---

'Love you too,' I reply.

My son gazes up at the darkening sky. His eyes grow wide as he strains to capture the disappearing sun. 'This is my favorite place in the whole world!' Stephen announces.

My throat becomes tight. A small stream of tears begins to fall. 'Mine too,' I reply. 'Mine too.'

Stephen is at that magical age of innocence, but yet is wise beyond his years. Even now, as salty tears run down my face, Stephen smiles, letting me maintain my dignity. But he knows why I'm crying. Stephen knows my tears are tears of joy.

'Love you Dad.'

'Love you too, son.'

I'm free.

As a child living in a dark world, I feared for my life and thought I was alone. As an adult I know now that I was not alone. There were thousands of other abused children.

Sources of information vary, but it is estimated that one in five children are physically, emotionally or sexually abused in the United States. Unfortunately, there are those among the uninformed public who believe that most abuse is nothing more than parents exerting their 'right' to discipline their children and letting it get a little out of hand. These same people may believe that over-discipline is not likely to follow the child into adulthood. They are tragically misinformed.

On any given day, some adult who is the victim of a dark past of child abuse may vent his or her pent-up frustrations on society or on those he or she may love. The public is well informed about the most uncommon cases. Unusual incidents attract the media and boost ratings. We heard about the lawyer father who struck out with his fist and left the child unconscious on the floor before retiring to bed. We heard about the father who dunked the small child in the toilet. Both children died. In a more bizarre case both a mother and a father each killed a child and hid their bodies for a period of four years. There are other high-profile stories, like the abused child who grew into the man who went on a killing spree at a McDonald's, gunning down helpless victims until the police took his life.

More common are the unknowns who disappear, like the homeless boy who sleeps under a freeway bridge and calls a cardboard box his home. Each year thousands of abused girls run away from home and sell their bodies in order to survive. Others strike out by joining gangs who are totally committed to violence and destruction.

Many child abuse victims hide their past deep inside, so deep that the possibility of becoming an abuser themselves is unthinkable. They live normal lives, becoming husbands and wives, raising families and building careers. But the ordinary problems of everyday life often force the former abuse victim to behave as they were taught as children. Spouses and children then become the object of their frustration, and they unknowingly come the full circle, completing the never-ending cycle of rage.

Some child abuse victims stay quietly locked in their shells. They look the other way, believing that by not acknowledging their past it will go away. They seem to believe that above all Pandora's Box must stay closed.

Each year, millions of dollars are poured into child protection agencies in the United States and around the world. These dollars go to local facilities like foster homes and juvenile halls. There are dollar grants to thousands of private organizations whose mission includes basic child abuse prevention, the counseling of abusive parents and the victims. Every year the number grows larger.

Why? What causes the tragedy of child abuse? Is it really as bad as they say? Can it be stopped? And perhaps the most important of all questions, what is abuse like through the eyes of the child?

What you have just read is a story of an ordinary

family that was devastated by their hidden secret. The story has two objectives: the first is to inform the reader how a loving, caring parent can change to a cold, abusive monster venting frustrations on a helpless child; the second is the eventual survival and triumph of the human spirit over seemingly insurmountable odds.

Some readers will find the story unreal and disturbing, but child abuse is a disturbing phenomenon that is a reality in our society. Child abuse has a domino effect that spreads to all who touch the family. It takes its greatest toll on the child and spreads into the immediate family to the spouse, who is often torn between the child and their mate. From there it goes to other children in the family who do not understand and also feel threatened. Also involved are neighbors who hear the screams but do not react, teachers who see the bruises and must deal with a child too distracted to learn, and relatives who want to intervene but do not want to risk relationships.

This is more than a story of survival. It is a story of victory and celebration. Even in its darkest passages, the heart is unconquerable. It is important that the body survives, but it is more meaningful that the human spirit prevails.

This is my story and mine alone. For years I was confined to the darkness of my own mind and heart, being alone and a pitiful 'loser'. At first I wanted nothing more than to be like others, but that motivation grew. I wanted to become a 'winner'. For over 13 years I served my country in the military. I now serve my country giving seminars and workshops to others in need, helping them to break their chains. From one who has been there, I bring a message to abused children and those who work with them. I bring a perspective born in the brutal reality of child abuse and nurtured in hope for a better tomorrow. Most importantly, I broke the cycle and became a father whose only guilt is that of spoiling his son with love and encouragement.

Today there are millions around the world in desperate need of help. It is my mission to assist those in need of a helping hand. I believe it is important for people to know that no matter what lies in their past, they can overcome the dark side and press on to a brighter world. It is perhaps a paradox that without the abuse of my past, I might not be what I am today.

———

Because of the darkness in my childhood, I have a deep appreciation for life. I was fortunate enough to turn tragedy into triumph. This is my story.

Perhaps at no time in history has the family been under more stress. Economic and social changes have pushed the family to its limit and made child abuse more likely. If society is to come to grips with the problem, it must be exposed. Once exposed, the causes of child abuse can be understood and support can truly begin. Childhood should be carefree, playing in the sun; not living a nightmare in the darkness of the soul.

# Steven E. Ziegler

### Teacher

September 1992 began as a typical back-to-school month for me. In my 22nd year of teaching, I found the usual hectic, non-stop confusion. There were close to 200 new students who had names for me to learn and several new faculty members to welcome aboard. It was goodbye to summer vacation and hello to additional responsibilities, and the annual doom and gloom from Sacramento regarding money for schools. Nothing had seemingly changed about the beginning of school, until a telephone message arrived on the 21st that rather painfully jolted me back 20 years: 'A David Pelzer would like you to contact his agent, regarding some child abuse reports you were associated with 20 years ago.' The past came back all too quickly.

Oh, yes, how well I remember David Pelzer. I was a recent college graduate, a new teacher; and as I look back, I realize I knew little about the real world of my chosen career. And the thing I knew least about was child abuse. In the early 1970s I didn't know if child abuse actually existed. If it did, it remained very much in the 'closet' as did so many unmentionable lifestyles and behaviors back then. We have learned so much; yet we have so far to go.

My mind returned to the Thomas Edison School in Daly City, California, September 1972. Enter little David Pelzer as one of my fifth-grade students. I was naive back then, but I was blessed with a sensitivity that told me there was something terribly wrong in David's life. Food missing from other students' lunches was traced to this thin, sad boy. Questionable bruises appeared on exposed parts of his body. Everything began to point to one thing: this kid was being beaten and punished in ways far beyond normal parental practice. It was several years later when I learned that what I was witnessing in my classroom was the third-worst case of child abuse on record in the entire state of California.

It is not for me to tell again all the graphic details my colleagues and I witnessed and reported to the authorities so many years ago. That account remains

David's privilege and opportunity in this book. But what a wonderful opportunity it is for this young man to come forward and tell his story so that other children may not suffer. I deeply admire his courage in doing so.

My very best to you, David. There is absolutely no doubt in my mind how far you have truly come.

If you would like to read more
of Dave Pelzer's compelling story,
here are extracts from the next two
volumes of his autobiography,
both published by Orion

## The Lost Boy

Available in paperback
£6·99

## A Man Named Dave

Available in paperback
£6·99

Also available

## Moving Forward

£6.99

# The Lost Boy

The inspiring sequel to
*A Child Called 'It'*

## Chapter 2
## An Angel Named Ms Gold

On 5 March 1973, I received the long-awaited answer to my prayers. I was rescued. My teachers and other staff members at Thomas Edison Elementary School intervened and notified the police.

Everything happened with lightning speed. I cried with all my heart as I said my final goodbyes to my teachers. I somehow knew I would never see them again. By the tears in their eyes I realized they understood the truth about me – the *real* truth. Why I was so different from the other children; why I smelled and dressed in rags; why I climbed into garbage cans to hunt for a morsel of food.

Before I left, my homeroom teacher, Mr Ziegler, bent down to say goodbye. He shook my hand and told me to be a good boy. He then whispered to me that he would tell my homeroom class the truth about me. Mr Ziegler's statement meant the world to me. I so badly wanted to be liked, to be accepted by my class, my school – by everyone.

The police officer had to nudge me through the door of the school office. 'Come on, David, we gotta go.' I wiped my nose before I stepped through the door. A million thoughts raced through my mind, all of them bad. I was terrified of what the consequences would be when Mother found out. No one had ever crossed The Mother like this before. When she found out, I knew there would be hell to pay.

As the police officer led me to his car, I could hear the sounds of all the schoolchildren playing in the yard during their lunch break. As we drove off, I twisted around in my seat to catch a glimpse of the schoolyard one last time. I left Thomas Edison Elementary School without having a single friend. But my only regret was that I did not have a chance to say goodbye to my English teacher, Mrs Woodworth, who was ill that day. During the time I was Mother's prisoner, Mrs Woodworth, without knowing, helped me escape my loneliness through the use of books. I had spent hundreds of hours in the dark, reading books of high adventure. This somehow eased my pain.

After filling out some forms at the police station, the officer called Mother to inform her that I was not coming home that afternoon, and that she could call the county's juvenile authorities if she had any questions. I sat like a statue, feeling both horror and excitement as the officer spoke on the phone. I could only imagine what was going through Mother's head. As the policeman spoke with a dry voice on the phone, I could see beads of sweat over his forehead. After he hung up the phone, I wondered for a moment if anyone else had ever had the same experience after talking to Mother. It seemed to be very important to the officer that we leave the station right away. I didn't help matters by pestering him over and over again as I jumped up and down and asked, 'What'd she say? What'd she say?' The officer refused to answer. He seemed to breathe easier once we drove past the city limits. He then bent down and said, 'David, you're free. Your mother is never going to hurt you again.'

I didn't fully understand the weight of his statement. I had hoped that he was taking me to some kind of jail, with all the other bad children – as Mother had programmed into me for so many years. I had decided long ago that I'd rather live in jail than live one more minute with *her*. I turned away from the sun. A single tear rolled down my face.

As long as I could remember, I had always wiped my tears and retreated inside my shell. This time I refused to wipe the tear away. I could feel the tear reach my lips, tasted the salt and let the tear dry on my skin as the rays from the sun baked through the windshield. I wanted to remember that tear not as a tear of fear, anger or sorrow, but as one of joy and freedom. I knew that from that moment on, everything in my life was new.

The officer drove me to the county hospital. Immediately, I was taken into an examination room. The nurse seemed shocked by my appearance. As gently as possible, she bathed my entire body from head to toe with a sponge before the doctor examined me. I couldn't look at her. I felt so ashamed as I sat on top of the cold metal examination table, wearing only my soiled underwear briefs filled with holes. As she washed my face, I turned away and kept my eyelids closed as tightly as I could. When the nurse finished, I gazed at the yellow-colored room filled with Snoopy cartoon characters. I looked down at different parts of my body. My legs and arms were a combination of yellow and brown. Dark circles of purple bruises faded on top of fresh rings of blue bruises – where I was either grabbed, punched or slammed down on the kitchen floor. When the doctor came into the room he seemed very concerned about my hands and arms. My fingers were dry, raw and red from all the years of using the combinations of cleaning chemicals used to complete my household chores. The doctor pinched the tips of my fingers, asking me if I could feel the pressure. I shook my head no. I hadn't been able to feel the tips of my fingers for some time now. He shook his head, claiming it was nothing to worry about, so I didn't think anything more of it.

Afterward, the police officer kindly led me through the maze of corridors as we made our way from room to room for lots of examinations, tests, blood samples and X-rays. I found myself moving in a daze. I felt as if I were watching someone else's life through my own eyes. I became so scared that I first asked, then begged the policeman to check around every corner and enter every room before I did. I knew that somewhere out there Mother was poised, ready to snatch me away. At first the officer refused, and only after I became so petrified that I couldn't breathe or move did the policeman humor me and follow my requests. I knew deep inside me heart that things were happening too fast – it was too easy for me to escape Mother.

Hours later we ended up with the same nurse who bathed me. She bent down to say something. I waited. She stared into my eyes, then after a few moments, she turned away. I could hear her sniffle. The doctor walked up behind me, patted my shoulder and gave me a bag containing cream for my hands. He then instructed me to keep my arms as clean as possible and said that it was too late to cover them. I looked at the officer, then down at my arms. I didn't under-stand. To me, my arms seemed the same as they always did – dark red with little skin. Both arms itched quite a bit, but that was normal for me. Before the policeman and I left, the doctor reached over and said to the officer, 'Make sure David gets plenty of food. And make sure he gets lots of time in the sun.' Then the doctor bent a little closer to him and asked, 'Where is she? You're not sending him back to his . . . ?'

The policeman locked eyes with the doctor. 'Not to worry, Doc. I gave this kid my word. His mother is *never* going to hurt him again.'

From that moment on, I knew I was safe. Standing near the officer, I wanted to hug his leg, but I knew I shouldn't. My eyes gleamed with joy. The police officer became my hero.

A few minutes after we left the hospital, he slowed his car as he drove through the hills on the narrow one-lane roads. I rolled down my window and stared in amazement at the sloping brown hills and tall redwood trees. Moments later the officer parked the car. 'Well, David, here we are.' I gazed down below me at the prettiest home I had ever seen. The officer explained that I would live here for a while and that this would be my new foster home. I had never heard the words *foster home* before, but I knew I would love the home. To me it seemed like a giant log cabin with lots of open windows. I could see that behind the home was a huge backyard, where sounds of screeching and laughter echoed by the tiny creek.

The elderly woman who ran the temporary foster home introduced herself as 'Aunt Mary' and greeted me at the kitchen door. I thanked the police officer with the strongest handshake I could. I felt bad that he had worked overtime for me. He knelt down and said in a deep voice, 'David, it's kids like you that made me want to become a policeman.' Without thinking, I grabbed his neck. The moment I did, my arms felt as if they were on fire. I didn't care. 'Thank you, sir.'

'Hey, kid, not a problem,' he replied. He then strolled up the curved walkway and saluted me from his car before driving off. I didn't even know his name.

After Aunt Mary fed me a delicious dinner of filet of sole, she introduced me to the seven other children who, like myself, for one reason or another no longer lived with their parents. I stared into every one of their faces. Some eyes were hollow, some full of worry, others full of confusion. I had no idea there were other unwanted children, too; for years I had felt I was all alone. At first I acted shy, but after a few questions from the other children, I opened up. 'What are you in for?' they asked. 'What happened to you?'

I bent my head down before replying that my mother didn't like me because I was always in trouble. I felt ashamed. I didn't want to tell them the secret about Mother and me. But none of that mattered to any of them, for I was just another face in the crowd. I was instantly accepted. I felt a surge of energy erupt from inside. From that moment on I became a wild child. I blitzed through the home as if my pants were on fire. I joked, laughed and screamed with joy, releasing years of solitude and silence.

I was uncontrollable. I ran from room to room, jumping from every mattress in the home. I bounced so high my head banged again and again against the ceiling. I didn't stop until I saw stars. I didn't care. The other children clapped their hands, egging me on. Their laughs were not cold, like the snide remarks reserved for me back at school, but were full of delight and approval.

My frolicking ended suddenly when I ran through the living room, nearly knocking over a lamp. By reflex, Aunt Mary grabbed my arm. She was about to scold me until she looked down at me. I covered my face, and my knees began to shake. Aunt Mary was a strict, elderly woman who stood her ground, but she didn't yell as she was known to do. For that evening my hyperactivity ended as quickly as air could escape balloon. Aunt Mary released her grip and knelt down, asking, 'What did she do to you?'

'I'm sorry,' I stuttered in a low voice. I was still unsure of Aunt Mary's intentions. I retreated into my protective position. 'I was a bad boy, and I deserved what I got!'

Later that evening Aunt Mary tucked me into bed. I began to cry, explaining to her that I was afraid Mother would come and take me away. She assured me I was safe and stayed with me until I felt secure. I stared up at the dark cedar ceiling. It reminded me of the old cabin in Guerneville. I fell asleep knowing that Mother was out there, somewhere, waiting to get me.

Alone in my dreams I found myself standing at the end of a long, dark hallway. A shadowy figure emerged at the opposite end. The figure transformed into *The Mother*. She began to march toward me. For some reason, I stood still. I couldn't move; I didn't even try. The closer The Mother came, the more her red face, filled with hatred, came into focus. The Mother held a shiny knife above her, poised and ready to strike me down. I turned and ran down the endless hallway. With all my strength I pumped my legs as fast as I could, searching for a light. I ran forever. The hallway twisted and turned as I hunted for an escape. I could feel The Mother's rancid breath on my neck and hear her cold voice chanting that there was no escape and that she would never let me go.

I snapped out of my dream. My face and chest were covered with a cold, sticky sweat. Not knowing if I was still dreaming, I covered my face. After my breathing began to slow down, I frantically looked all around. I was still in the cedar room. I still had on a pair of pajamas that Aunt Mary had loaned me. I patted myself, feeling for any wounds. *A dream*, I told myself. *A bad dream, that's all.* I tried to control my breathing but couldn't shake the vision. The Mother's words echoed in my mind: '*I will never let you go. Never!*'

I jumped out of bed and scrambled around in the darkness to throw on my clothes. I returned to the head of the bed and held my knees close to my chest. I couldn't go back to sleep. That's where The Mother now lived – in my dreams. I felt it was a mistake that I was taken away, and I knew I would soon be returned to her. That night, and those to follow, while everyone slept, I held on to my knees as I rocked backed and forth, humming to myself. I would stare through the window and listen to the trees sway in the evening breeze. I told myself that I would never fall into the nightmare again.

My first encounter with the county's Child Protective Service agency came in the form of an angel named Ms Gold. Her long, shiny blond hair and bright face matched her name. 'Hi,' she smiled. 'I'm your social worker.' And so began the long and drawn-out sessions in which I had to explain things I did not totally understand. In the beginning of our first session, I huddled at the far end of the couch while Ms Gold sat at the other end. Without my knowing, she slowly inched her way toward me until she was close enough to hold my hand. At first I was too scared to have her touch me. I did not deserve her kindness. But Ms Gold held on to my hand, caressing my palm, assuring me that she was there to help me. That day she stayed with me for over five hours.

The other visits were just as long. At times I was too scared to talk and long moments of silence followed. Other times, for no apparent reason and not under-standing why, I'd burst into tears. Ms Gold didn't care. She simply held me tight and rocked me back and forth, whispering in my ear that everything was going to be all right. Sometimes we would lie at the end of the couch, and I would talk about things that were of no relation to my bad past. During those times I would play with the long strands of Ms Gold's shiny hair. I'd lie in her arms and breathe in the fragrance of her flowery perfume. I soon began to trust Ms Gold.

She became my best friend. After school, whenever I saw her car, I'd sprint down the walkway and burst into Aunt Mary's home, knowing Ms Gold had come to see me. We always ended our sessions with a long hug. She would then bend down and assure me that I did not deserve to be treated the way I was and that what my mother did to me was not my fault. I had heard Ms Gold's words before, but after years of brainwashing I wasn't so sure. So much had happened so fast. One time I asked Ms Gold why she needed all of this information on Mother and me. To my horror, she told me that the county was going to use it against my mother. 'No!' I pleaded. 'She must never know I told you! *Never!*'

Ms Gold assured me that I was doing the right thing, but when she left me alone to think, I came to a different conclusion. As long as I could remember, I had always been in trouble. I was always being punished for one thing or another. Whenever my parents had fought, my name was always thrown into the ring. Was it really Mother's fault? Maybe I deserved everything I got over the years. I did lie and steal food. And I knew I was the reason why Mother and Father no longer lived together. Would the county throw Mother in jail? Then what would happen to my brothers? That day after Ms Gold left, I sat alone on the couch. My mind raced with questions. I felt my insides turn to jelly. *My God! What have I done?*

Days later, on a Sunday afternoon, while I was outside learning to play basketball, I heard the old familiar sound of Mother's station wagon. My heart felt as though it stopped beating. I closed my eyes, thinking I was daydreaming. When my brain responded, I turned and ran inside Aunt Mary's home and smashed into her. 'It's ... it's my ...' I stuttered.

'Yes, I know,' Aunt Mary gently spoke as she held me. 'You're going to be all right.'

'No! You don't under ... she's going to take me away! She found me!' I yelled. I tried to squirm myself away from Aunt Mary's grip so I could run outside and find a safe place to hide.

Aunt Mary's grip didn't budge. 'I didn't want to upset you,' Aunt Mary said. 'She's just going to drop off some clothes. You're going to court this Wednesday, and your mother wants you to look nice.'

'No!' I cried. 'She's going to take me! She's going to take me back!'

'David, be still! I'll be right here if you need me. Now, please be still young man!' Aunt Mary did her best to calm me down. But my eyes nearly popped out as I watched The Mother stroll down the walkway with *her* four boys in tow.

I sat by Aunt Mary's side. Greetings were exchanged, and like a trained dog I became my old self – the child called 'It'. In an instant I went from an enthusiastic boy to Mother's invisible house slave.

Mother didn't even acknowledge my presence. Instead, she turned to Aunt Mary. 'So, tell me, how is *The Boy*?'

I looked up at Aunt Mary's face. She seemed startled. Her eyes flickered for just a second. '*David*? David is quite fine, thank you. He's right here, you know,' Aunt Mary responded, holding me a little tighter.

'Yes,' Mother said in a dry voice, 'I can see that.' I could feel Mother's hate burn through me. 'And how does he get along with the other children?'

Aunt Mary cocked her head to one side. 'Quite fine. *David* is very polite and extremely helpful around the home. He's always looking to help out,' she answered, knowing that Mother had no intention of talking to me directly.

'Well ... you should be careful,' Mother warned. 'He's tried to hurt other children. He does not get along well with others. *The Boy* is violent. He needs special attention, discipline that only I know how to instill. You don't know *The Boy*.'

I could feel the muscles on Aunt Mary's arm become tight as a drum. She leaned forward, giving Mother her best smile – the kind of smile that Aunt Mary would like to slap Mother silly with. '*David* is a fine young man. *David* may be a bit rambunctious ... but that's to be expected considering what *David*'s been put through!'

Suddenly I realized what was happening. Mother was trying to gain control over Aunt Mary, and Mother was losing. On the outside my shoulders slumped forward, and I gave Mother my timid puppy dog look as I stared down at the carpet. But on the inside my ears became like radar, picking up every phrase, every syllable of the conversation. *Finally*, I said to myself. *Someone has finally put Mother in her place. Yes!*

The more I heard Aunt Mary's tone change toward Mother, the more my face lit up. I was enjoying this. I slowly lifted my head up. I looked right into Mother's eyes. Inside I smiled. *Well, isn't this nice. It's about time*, I said to myself. As I listened to them, my head began to weave from left to right, then back again, as if I were watching a tennis match. Aunt Mary tried again to have Mother acknowledge me. I nodded my head at Mother as I openly agreed with Aunt Mary.

I began to feel extremely confident. *I* am *someone. I* am *somebody*, I told myself. I could feel parts of my body begin to relax. I was no longer scared. For once, everything was fine – right up until the moment I heard the phone ring. My head snapped to the right as the kitchen phone shrilled. I counted the rings, hoping someone would hang up. I became tense after the 12th ring. Aunt Mary turned toward the kitchen. I grabbed her arm. *Come on*, I said to myself. *No one's home. Just hang up.* But the phone kept ringing – 16, 17, 18 times. *Just hang up! Just hang up!* I could feel Aunt Mary lean forward to get up. I kept my hand on her arm, trying to force her to stay. When she stood up, I followed. My right hand clamped onto her left arm. She stopped midstride and pried my hand off, finger by finger.

'David, please. It's just the phone. For goodness sake, don't be rude. Now go back in there.' I stood still. I locked onto Aunt Mary's eyes for a brief moment. Aunt Mary understood. She nodded her head. 'Okay,' she said in a low voice. 'Come on, you can stay with me.'

I let out a sigh of relief as I followed her feet to the kitchen. Suddenly, I felt my left arm being yanked backwards. I nearly lost my footing. I fought to regain my balance. I closed my eyes as I bit my lip. My legs began to shake. Inches in front of me sat Mother. Her heavy, raspy breathing made me quiver. Mother's face was dark red. I could tell that from behind her glasses her eyes were on fire. I tried to search for my savior, but Aunt Mary had already turned into the kitchen.

I stared down at the carpet, wishing her away. Mother squeezed my arm tighter. 'Look at me!' she hissed. I became frozen. I wanted to yell, but my voice became mute. Her evil eyes locked onto mine. I closed my eyes as I felt Mother's head inch its way toward my face. Mother's monotone voice became vicious. 'Cocky little bastard, aren't you? Well, you don't look so tall now. Do you? What's the matter? Has your little Aunt Mary left you?' she said in a sarcastic, whining voice.

Mother then yanked me so close to her face that I could smell her breath and feel droplets of saliva spray on my face. Mother's voice turned ice cold. 'Do you know what in the hell you've done? Do you?! The questions they've asked me? Do you realize the embarrassment you've cost *This Family*?' Mother asked, as she spread her left hand at my brothers sitting beside her.

My knees began to buckle. I wanted to go to the bathroom and throw up. Mother smiled, showing me her dark yellow teeth. 'They think I tried to hurt you. Now why would I do that?'

I tried to turn my head toward the kitchen. I could barely make out Aunt Mary's voice on the phone.

'Child!' Mother hissed, 'Boy ... get this straight! I don't care what they say! I don't care what they do! You're not out of this yet! I'll get you back! You hear me? *I'll get you back!*'

When she heard Aunt Mary hang up the phone, Mother released my arm and pushed me away. I sat back in the wide chair and watched my savior stroll back into the living room and sit down beside me. 'I'm sorry about that,' Aunt Mary said.

Mother batted her eyes and waved her hand.

Suddenly she became regal. The act was on. 'That? Oh, the phone? No problem. I have to . . . I mean, we have to get going anyway.'

I stole a glance at my brothers. Their eyes were hard and fixed. I gazed at them, wondering what they thought of me. Except for Kevin, who was still a toddler, the three of them seemed as if they wanted to throw me outside and stomp on me. I knew they hated me, and I felt I deserved it. For I had exposed the family secret.

I tried to imagine what it must be like for them to live with Mother now. I prayed that somehow my brothers would forgive me. I felt like a deserter. I also prayed that the cycle of hate had not moved on to one of them. I felt sorry for them. They had to live in total hell.

After another round of pleasantries and final warnings from Mother to Aunt Mary, *The Family* departed. As I heard the sound of Mother's tires from her station wagon mash down on the rocks as she drove away, I remained glued to the chair. I sat in the living room for the rest of the afternoon, rocking back and forth, repeating Mother's pledge over and over again, '*I'll get you back. I'll get you back.*'

That evening I couldn't eat. In bed I rolled back and forth until I sat up, clutching my knees. The Mother was right. I knew in my heart she would get me back. I stared out the window of my room. I could hear the wind howl through the tops of trees and the branches rub against each other. My chest began to tighten. I cried. I knew at that moment there was no escape for me.

At school the next day I couldn't concentrate on my work. I strolled around the schoolyard like a zombie. Later that afternoon I met Ms Gold at Aunt Mary's home. 'David, we're going to court in two days. I need to ask you just a few questions to clarify our case. Okay, honey?' she asked with a bright smile.

I refused to speak and sat rigidly at the far end of the couch. I couldn't look at Ms Gold. To her dismay I muttered, 'I don't think I should say anything.'

Ms Gold's mouth nearly fell to the carpet. She began to speak, but I raised my hand, cutting her off. I then retracted as many statements as I could, claiming that I had lied about everything. I had caused all of the household problems. I told her that I had fallen down the stairs. I had run into doorknobs. I had beaten myself. I had stabbed myself. I then cried to Ms Gold that my mommy was a beautiful, kind woman, with the perfect flower garden, the perfect home, the perfect family, and that I craved her attention because of my other brothers. And everything was all my fault.

Ms Gold became speechless. She scooted over to where I sat. She tried several times to reach out and hold my hand. I brushed her delicate fingers away. She became so frustrated that she began to cry. After several hours and many attempts, Ms Gold looked at me with dried streaks of tears and blotches of black eyeliner running down her face. 'David, honey,' she sniffed. 'I don't understand. Why won't you talk to me? Please, honey.'

Then she tried to switch tactics. She stood up and pointed her finger at me. 'Don't you know how important this case is? Don't you know that all I talk about in my office is a cute little boy who is brave enough to tell me his secret?'

I looked through Ms Gold and tuned her out. 'I don't think I should say anything else,' I coldly replied.

Ms Gold bent over, trying to force me to look into her face. 'David, please . . .' she begged.

But to me, she just wasn't there. I knew that my social worker was trying everything in her power to help me, but I feared Mother's wrath more than Ms Gold's. From the moment Mother stated 'I'll get you back,' I knew everything in my new world was lost.

Ms Gold reached out to hold my hand. I slapped her fingers away. I turned my back to her. 'David James Pelzer!' she barked. 'Do you have any idea what you're saying? Do you understand what you're doing? You had better get your story straight! You're going to have to make a major decision pretty soon, and you better be ready for it!'

Ms Gold sat back down, wedging me between her knees and the end of the couch. 'David, you have to understand that in a person's life there are a few precious moments in which decisions, choices that you make now, will affect you for the rest of your life. I can help you, but only if you let me. Do you understand?'

I again turned away. Suddenly Ms Gold sprang up from the couch. Her face became bright red and her hands were shaking. I tried to hold back my feelings, but a surge of anger erupted. 'No!' I cried out. 'Don't you get it? Don't you understand? She'll get me back. She'll win. She always wins. No one can stop The Mother. Not you, not anyone! She'll get me back!'

———

Her face went blank. 'Oh my God!' Ms Gold exclaimed as she bent down to hold me. 'Is that what she said to you? David, honey . . .' Her arms stretched out to embrace me.

'No!' I yelled. 'Won't you just leave me alone? Just . . . go . . . away!'

Ms Gold stood over me for a few moments, then turned on her heels and stormed out of the room. A few seconds later I could hear the sound of the screen door slamming in the kitchen. Without thinking, I ran into the kitchen, but I stood frozen behind the door. Through the screen I could see Ms Gold stumbling up the steep walkway. She lost her grip on her papers and tried to catch some of them in midair. 'Shit!' she cried out. The papers scattered as she desperately tried to gather them into one pile. As soon as she stood up, she fell down, scraping her right knee. I could see the frustration on her face as she clamped her hand over her mouth. Ms Gold tried again to stand up, but this time with more caution as she made her way to the county car. She slammed the car door shut and bent her head against the steering wheel. As I stood behind the screen door, I could hear Ms Gold – my angel –

sobbing uncontrollably. After several minutes she finally started her car and sped off.

I stayed behind the kitchen screen and cried inside. I knew I could never forgive myself, but lying to Ms Gold was the lesser of two evils. I stood alone, confused, behind the screen door. I felt that by lying, I had protected Mother, that I had done the right thing. I knew Mother was going to get me back and no one could stop her. But then when I thought of how kind Ms Gold had been throughout everything, I suddenly realized the terrible position I had just put her in. I never meant to hurt anybody, especially Ms Gold. I became a statue as I stood behind the screen door. I only wished that I could crawl under a rock and hide, forever.

# A Man Named Dave

The heartwarming conclusion
to Dave Pelzer's story

## Chapter 2
## *Fly Away*

24 *August 1979*

Thick, sticky sweat coated every pore of my skin. My stomach seized with fear. My fingers seemed fused together as they clawed the armrest. I wanted to shut my eyes, but the combination of exhilaration, fascination, and terror inside me kept them glued to the small Plexiglas window. I studied every feature of the Bay Area – my home for the last eighteen years.

'I'm flying?' I asked, to my own amazement.

My body slid from my seat, and I thought for sure I'd fall out of the plane as the Boeing 727 made a sudden sharp roll to the right. To help contain my fear, I forced my eyes shut. *I'm okay. I'm all right. I'm fine. My god, I can't believe it! I'm flying! I'm actually flying!* I could feel myself drifting off. Because of the excitement of finally enlisting in the U.S. Air Force, saying goodbye to my foster parents, and struggling with my past, I had not slept in days. As the roar of the jet's engines began to fade, I started to unwind. The more my tension disappeared, the more I began to think of how far I had come.

As a child surviving in the garage of Mother's house, I had never dreamed of making it out alive. Somehow, I had known Mother was close to killing me, and yet I did not care. I had given up all hope. Yet on 5 March 1973, the day after Mother had thrown me down the garage stairs, my teachers called the police, who immediately placed me into protective custody. I was free. As elated as I was, I sensed that my freedom was a hollow victory. At the county's court proceedings, I felt that Mother had given me away. I felt as if *I* was not good enough for *her*. When my angel of mercy – my social worker, Ms Gold – informed me that I was never to have any contact with Mother or her children ever again, I was crushed.

It was then that I became obsessed with finding answers to my past. Even though I was still terrified of Mother, who wanted nothing to do with me, I still struggled to prove that I was worthy of her love and worthy enough to be a member of her family.

As a foster child, I soon learned that I knew

absolutely nothing about *living in the real world.* My former life as Mother's prisoner had been dominated by elemental needs of survival. But after my rescue I felt like a toddler – learning and growing by leaps and bounds. The simplest things taught to preschool children became major obstacles for me. Because I had spent years in the garage with my head bent backward in a POW position, I developed very bad posture. As a foster child, I had to learn to focus and walk upright. Whenever I became nervous, I stuttered or slurred every word. It would take me forever to complete one simple sentence. My foster mother, Mrs Turnbough, spent hours with me every day after school, teaching me phonics and helping me to imagine my words flowing from my mouth, like water cascading over a fall. Mrs Turnbough's valiant efforts were perhaps her undoing. Within a few months, I was driving my foster parents up the wall with all I had to say. They had all they could do to shut me up. I wanted to show off my new form of communication to everyone, every minute. But my mouth soon became my Achilles' heel. Because I was so skinny and awkward, I became easy prey for others, and my only form of defense was my mouth. Whenever I felt backed in a corner, words of intense anger and hatred seemed to erupt before I could analyze what I was saying or why.

The only way I felt I could make friends was stealing for acceptance or doing whatever else I could to gain recognition. I knew that what I was doing was completely wrong, but after years of being an outcast and totally isolated, the need to fit in was too powerful to resist. My foster parents struggled to keep me on the straight and narrow, and teach me the seriousness of my decisions.

On the lighter side, they were dismayed at my naïveté and ignorance. The first few times I took a bath, I filled the tub to the rim *before* stepping into it, causing water to spill over the sides. I would then squeeze every drop I could from what I thought was 'fancy-smelling bubble bath' into the tub, then stir the water like a whirlpool trying to form as much lather as possible. As much as my foster parents laughed at my water frolics, my foster sisters were not amused and hid their bottles of Vidal Sassoon in their bedrooms. Up until then I had never heard of the word shampoo.

I thought that in order to survive, I had to work. Early on as a foster child, it was drummed into me that foster kids – labeled as 'F-kids' – never amounted to anything, never graduated high school, let alone go on to college. I also discovered that by the time I turned eighteen years old, I would no longer be a ward of the court – a minor that was provided for by the county – and since I didn't have parents to rely on, I would be all alone. The closer I came to reaching adulthood, the more I became terrified of being broke and homeless. Deep down I feared I would not be strong enough to make it on my own. As a frightened child living in my mother's garage, one of the promises I had made was that if I ever escaped, I would always have enough money to eat. So, as a young teenager, I abandoned my Lego and Erector sets and my Hot Wheels toy cars and focused on earning a living. By the age of fifteen I was shining shoes. I lied about my age to get work as a busboy. I did whatever I could to put in at least forty hours a week. As a freshman in high school, I slaved six days a week to put in over sixty hours. I did anything I could to squeeze in an extra hour a week to earn an additional $2.65. Only after I'd show up to school and collapse on top of my desk and get sick from total exhaustion did I begin to slack off. On one level, thinking that I was ahead of the game, I was proud, almost to the point of being cocky. But on the inside I felt hollow and lonely. As other boys my age were dating beautiful girls with short dresses and fancy makeup, driving their parents' cars and whining about their ten-hour work weeks, I became increasingly jealous of their good fortune.

Whenever I felt a little depressed, I would bury myself even more in my work. The harder I applied myself, the more the cravings of wanting to be a normal teenager disappeared. And more important, the inner voice bubbling inside me, fighting for the answers to my past, remained quiet.

For me, work meant peace.

In the summer of 1978, at age eighteen, in order to further my career as top-rated car salesman, I decided to drop out of high school. But months later, after a statewide recession, I found myself as a legal adult, with no diploma, no job, and my life savings quickly draining away. My worst nightmare had come true. All of my well-thought-out plans of getting ahead and sacrificing while others played vanished into thin air. Because of my lack of education, the only jobs available were at fast-food restaurants. I knew I could not make it by working those jobs for the rest of my life.

Ever since I had been Mother's prisoner, I had dreamed of making something of myself. The more she would scream, curse at me, and leave me sprawled out on the floor in my own blood, the more I would fight back and smile inside, telling myself over and over again, *One day, you'll see. One of these days I'll make you proud.* But Mother's prediction was right: I had failed. And for that I hated myself to the core. My idle time awakened my inner voice. I began to think that maybe Mother had been right all along. Maybe I was a loser, and I had been treated as such because I deserved it. I became so paranoid about my future that I could no longer sleep. I spent my free evenings trying to form any strategy I could to survive. It was during one of those endless nights that I remembered the only piece of advice my father ever gave me.

In six years as a foster child, I had seen my father less than a dozen times. At the end of my last visit, he proudly showed me one of the only possessions he had left: his badge, representing his retirement from the San Francisco Fire Department. Before loading me onto a Greyhound bus, Father mumbled in a dejected voice, 'Get out of here, David. Get as far away from here as you can. You're almost at that age. Get out.' As he looked at me with darkened circles under his eyes, Father's final words were: 'Do what you have to. Don't end up ... don't end up like me.'

In my heart I sensed that Father was a homeless alcoholic. After spending a lifetime saving others from burning buldings, Father had been helpless to save himself. That day as the bus pulled away, I cried from the depths of my soul. Every time the bus passed someone sleeping beside a building, I'd imagine Father shivering in the night. As much as I felt sorry for him, though, I knew I did not want to – I could not – end up like him. I felt selfish thinking of myself rather than my stricken father, but his advice, *Don't end up like me*, became my personal commandment.

I decided that joining the service was my only chance. I even fantasized about serving in the air force as a fireman, then one day returning to the Bay Area and showing Father my badge. Trying to enlist proved to be an ordeal. After struggling to obtain my GED, I had to fill out mounds of paperwork for every time I had been bounced from one foster home to another, then explain on separate forms why I was placed in another home. Whenever the air force recruiter pressed me about my past, I became so terrified that I stuttered like an idiot. After weeks of evading these questions, I caved in and gave the sergeant a brief explanation about why Mother and I did not get along. I waited for his reaction. I held my breath knowing that if the recruiter thought I was a troublemaker, he would refuse my application.

Every morning, for weeks, I stood outside the door, waiting for the office to open, before I hurried in to fill out more paperwork, and studied films and whatever booklets the recruiter had available. I became possessed to enlist. The air force was my ticket to a new life.

After the paperwork was filled out, double-checked, then reverified, I had to get a physical examination. During the battery of tests I was poked and prodded on every inch of my rail-thin body. At the end, as I sat nearly naked, the doctor kept circling around me as he questioned the ancient bumps on my scalp, the scars on my body, the marks on my right arm where Mother had burned me on the gas stove. I simply shrugged off the doctor's questions, telling him I had been a clumsy kid. The doctor let out a sigh and raised his eyebrows. Immediately my heart seized. I just knew I had said the wrong thing. Fearing my statement would disqualify me, I quickly added that it was a stage I had gone through when I was a kid. 'A kid?' the doctor asked, as if he were not buying my story.

'Yeah, you know, when I was six, seven years old. But' – I raised a finger to stress the importance of this point – 'I'm not clumsy now! Nope, not anymore. Not me. No sireee . . .' The doctor waved me off and told me to get dressed. I felt a surge of relief as I saw him mark the block that claimed I was medically qualified to enlist. I was on top of the world, right up until the moment I leaned too far and crashed against the table. Folders containing other recruits' paperwork exploded in every direction, and, still struggling to pull on my pants, I tried to grab the papers, only scattering them more. The doctor ordered me to stop trying to help and get out of his office as fast as humanly possible. As I hurried out the door, the doctor flashed a smile. 'Over that clumsy period, eh?'

Hours later that same day, I sat frozen in front of a computer next to an air force sergeant who typed in an endless stream of information. Finally, the sergeant paused, turned toward me, and nonchalantly asked, 'So, what day do you want to enlist?'

I shook my head, not sure I had heard what the sergeant just asked. I leaned forward and whispered, 'You mean, I'm in? I can join? You're actually asking me if I want to join?'

'Don't make a federal case out of it. Yeah, you're in – that is, unless the FBI tells us you're a criminal,' the sergeant teased.

My mind immediately flashed back to all the close calls I had had with the police for speeding tickets when I was a teenager. My heart skipped a beat. I knew that if the air force found out about my past, I was a goner. The sergeant startled me when he tapped on my shoulder. 'Hey, Pelz-ter, relax. So . . . when do you want to enlist?'

I was lost in a daze. *Now you have the chance to make something of yourself. Now is your time to build a life.* I simply could not believe that after struggling over six months, I had actually made it.

I allowed myself the reward of smiling. 'When's the soonest I can join?'

He snapped back, 'Girlfriend problems, eh?' Before I had a chance to respond, the man bowed his head and feverishly pounded on the computer keyboard. 'Well,' he began, 'if you really feel the need for speed, I can have you on a plane and in basic training by . . . tonight. Or, if that doesn't suit you, you can enlist next week. So, what will it be?'

I immediately knew what I had to do, but a wave of shame washed over me. For months I had lied to my foster parents, telling them that I was taking specialized tests and interviewing for a job, which in a way I felt I was. The Turnboughs had no idea what I was really up to. I felt a sudden urge to run off and enlist and then simply phone them from boot camp. Besides my foster parents and a handful of close friends, I had no one in my life. No girlfriends, no work buddies, no friends who picked me up to go cruising or see movies, no relatives to speak of – no one. I felt that if I fell off the face of the earth, less than half a dozen people would even notice. But deep in my heart I knew that I owed my *real* family – my foster parents and whatever friends I had – more than a long-distance phone call. Above all, it was a matter of honor. I let out a deep sigh before answering the sergeant. 'Next week.'

'All right, next week. You sure about this?' he politely asked.

Without blinking an eye, I nodded my head. 'Yes, sir!'

The sergeant pressed a button, and the computer began printing a stream of papers. 'Sign here, here, here, here and ... here,' he informed me without a trace of emotion. I stared at the blocks with the bright red Xs. *This is it!* I told myself. I snatched the government pen and scribbled my name so hard that I nearly tore through the sheets of paper. As the sergeant took the paperwork and typed in more commands to his computer, I killed time by looking at the framed glossy photographs of the high-tech air force fighter jets. My mouth began to water at the sleek, crisp lines of the airplanes against the endless blue sky.

'Sir, is that the F-15 jet fighter?' I asked, pointing at a photograph above his desk.

Without looking up from the computer, the sergeant replied, 'Nope ... F-16.'

I nodded my head to the sergeant's answer, then stated before thinking, 'Excuse me, sir, but if I'm not mistaken, that's the McDonnell Douglas F-15 Eagle: first strike, air superior fighter, capable of speeds in excess of Mach 2.5, produced by a pair of G.E. F-100 after-burning engines. . . .'

The sergeant turned toward me with his mouth hung open.

'Did I say something wrong, sir?' I thought for a moment of what I had just said, and even I was surprised how easy the basic technical aspects of the airplane came from my mouth. All these facts I had learned from the recruitment brochures and stream of books I had digested over the last few months.

He simply nodded for me to continue.

Immediately I thought this was part of some strange test. I closed my eyes to recall as much as I could. 'Uhm, I know it has a comple . . . dent – I mean, complement of AIM-7 Sparrow and AIM-9 Side-winder missiles. And . . . I think . . . it was two, maybe three years ago that a modified F-15 Streak Eagle beat the time-to-climb altitude record held by a Russian MeG.' I paused to catch my breath and waited for his reaction. Craving acceptance, I didn't want the sergeant to think I was trying to show off. By the smile in his eyes I realized he was not only impressed, but interested in planes as well.

'That's "MiG" Pelz-ter, not "MeG," ' he countered.

'Okay, smart guy: What base did they launch the Streak Eagle from?'

'Grand Forks, North Dakota!' I stated with confidence.

'All right, not bad. Now,' he said, 'the big one: Why Grand Forks?'

I smiled back, enjoying the game. 'Molecule compression. The colder air allows the plane to reach speeds and altitudes quicker while at the same time consuming less fuel. I mean . . . I think that's the idea.'

The sergeant responded with a wide grin and slapped me on the shoulder. 'Where in the hell did you . . . ?'

By instinct, I hesitated. For a second I thought I had just revealed military secrets. 'I read, sir.'

'You read?'

'Ah . . . yes, sir. I read a lot. I've always wanted to . . . I mean, Sergeant?' I asked in a low voice. 'You think they'd ever let me fly?'

'My Lord!' He coughed. 'You're a piece of work, aren't you?

'Hey, Max,' he bellowed to the next cubicle. 'I got the next Chuck Yeager over here! Wants to know if he can fly!' As a small roar of laughter erupted, I closed my eyes. I always seemed to say the wrong thing at the wrong time and make a jerk out of myself.

After I let out a deep breath, the sergeant caught my eye. I stated in a firm tone, 'Chuck Yeager was *enlisted* before he flew.'

The sergeant thumbed through my paperwork. 'Listen, Pelz, you barely made it in. You're a high school dropout, your aptitude scores are *way* below average, and you have the body of a skinny rat with the eyesight of Stevie Wonder. A fly boy? Thought you wanted to be a fireman. Listen,' he said, 'here's what you do: Learn your trade as a fireman and get some college classes under your belt. Heck, the air force will pay for your tuition. And then after a few years if you want to reenlist, you can apply for a slot. That's a major goal, but if you're serious, we'll meet you halfway. Okay?'

I swallowed hard, realizing how lucky I was to even enlist. 'Yes, sir. I understand. Thanks for the advice.'

'Hey, that's what I'm here for.' He stood up, indicating he was through with me. 'Not to worry, Pelz. You keep studying and they'll have you piloting the SR-71.' He then raised his eyebrows. 'I assume with your plethora of aeronautical knowledge, you do know about the Blackbird, *don't you?'*

My eyes lit up at the mention of my favorite plane. 'Yes, sir!' I exclaimed. 'I know about the Blackbird, like nobody's business!'

'Well then, we'll see you next week.' He extended his hand.

'Thank you, sir,' I said as I shook it. 'I'll make you proud. You'll see.'

The sergeant let out a chuckle, released my hand, then snapped to attention and gave me a crisp salute. 'See ya, *Airman Pelz-a-Yeager!'*

Later that afternoon, before I chickened out and changed my mind, I informed my foster parents, 'I enlisted in the air force! I leave next week!'

'Oh, really?' my foster father, Harold Turnbough, casually replied.

I searched their eyes for any kind of reaction to my explosive news. After what seemed like an eternity of silence, I broke the ice. 'I'm going nowhere. I've been working myself stupid. I thought I could find the answers – to my past, to Mother – trying to numb myself about my dad. And now, now it's my time. My time to make something of myself. I've already missed so much, but if I stay focused and work hard, maybe someday I can turn this around.' I stopped to gauge their response. My foster parents continued to just sit there. 'Isn't that what you've tried to teach me; I mean, to become self-reliant? Well...?' I asked, frustrated.

Alice and Harold, who years ago had adopted me into their hearts, began to nod their heads before exploding with laughter. I shook my head in disgust. Because of the day's mounting tensions – the test and examinations, my fear of not being good enough to enlist, my lack of sleep, and hiding my secret for so long – I felt sick to my stomach. 'Stop it!' I shouted. 'What's so funny? This is serious! I mean it! I already signed the paperwork.'

Alice leaned over to embrace me. 'We've known for a while, David.'

Harold said with a crooked smile, 'With all those brochures layin' around and your babblin' 'bout airplanes this, airplanes that, what else would you be up to?'

'So, you're not mad? I mean...?'

'Of course not, David. But answer this: Why the service? Three years is a long time,' said Alice.

'Four years; I'll be in for four,' I corrected her. 'I'm just fed up. I'm tired of living hand to mouth. Working my butt off, for what? For nothing! I've been scrimping and slaving away, and I have nothing to show for it. Check it out: In four years I can grow and learn, I can explore and see things beyond any picture of any magazine.' I stopped and lowered my head. 'Maybe getting away will help me . . . help me find my answers. . . .'

Mrs Turnbough reached over to cup my hand. 'David, you may never know. Sometimes, bad things happen. For some things there are no absolutes.'

'No,' I interrupted, 'it's wrong. I have to know. I have to find out. If I don't deal with this, all I'm doing is hiding "the secret" like everyone else, and if I do that, then what's to say I don't become like her or like my dad? Something made them the way they are. Things do happen for a reason. I want to understand; I want to know. And if I don't find out and do something, who will? How many kids have you taken in who came from the same kind of home as me? The problem's not going to go away by turning our backs or sweeping it underneath the carpet anymore. Every day *things* happen, and everyone acts as if nothing's wrong. No one wants to talk about *things*, let alone deal with the consequences afterward. It's wrong, and it's about time to take a stand. Isn't that what you and everyone else has pounded into my head since I was rescued? Be good, be honest and fair, find something I believe in, work hard and keep the faith no matter how long it takes? Well . . . ?'

My foster parents sat in front of me totally mesmerized. In all the years I had known them, they had never seen me so intense, so articulate about my past. I continued in a softer tone. 'Listen, it's going to be okay, I can handle it. I'll be fine, but please understand, I don't want to turn out like them. This is something *I've* got to do.'

I took a moment to compose my thoughts. I did not want to screw up and tell them in the wrong way what I felt in my heart. 'You know I love you both very much. You've treated me as if I were a *real* person. But while I'm in the air force, I'm gonna save every dollar I can. I want a home . . . *my home*. I want to buy a home in Guerneville, on the Russian River. Ever since kindergarten, I knew that's what I wanted. That's my lifelong dream. When I lived in Mother's house, when things were really bad, I'd go outside and dream of a log home by the river with a warm fireplace and the smell of redwood trees. It made me feel safe. Of all the things she did to me, Mother could never get me when I thought about the river. As a kid, that dream gave me something to live for. I want *my* home.' I hesitated as my throat tightened. Tears began to trickle down the sides of my face. I tried to hold back my emotions, but the years of extreme pressure were just too much.

'David, what is it? What's wrong?' Mrs Turnbough whispered.

I closed my eyes before bursting with a flood of tears. 'All his life, all he wanted was to have something... And now he's alone, living on the streets, and has nothing. It's not right.'

'Who's alone? Who are you talking about?' Alice probed.

'My father!' I cried. 'I'm gonna buy a house and have Dad live with me. It's the right thing to do. And,' I said, renewing my vow, 'I'm going to find my answers, and when I'm ready, I'm going to do what I can to make a difference.' I wiped my tears away, feeling foolish.

'So, you're joining the air force?' Harold asked with a hint of humor. 'Do you think you can manage to stay out of *the brig*?'

My smile matched Harold's. 'Yes, sir!' I said. 'I'll make you proud, you watch. One day, you'll see. I'll make you proud!'

'Well,' Alice broke in, 'now that you've made your decision, when are you going to tell your parents?'

I took a long, deep breath. As I inhaled, I felt clean. I could feel my entire body relax. I suddenly felt as if I could curl up in a big, soft bed and sleep forever. For the first time in nearly half a year I found myself at peace. In front of me the Turnboughs sat hand in hand. I gently placed my hands around theirs. 'As far as I'm concerned, *Mom*,' I said as I gazed into Alice's eyes, '*and Dad*,' I said, looking at Harold, 'I've enlisted in the United States Air Force. I leave next week. Any questions?'

The Boeing 727's sudden downward lurch shook me from my trance. I blinked, struggling to focus on the San Antonio skyline outside the airplane window. The more I stared through the Plexiglas, the more the faces and serenity of my parents faded away. I was on the threshold of my new life. I took a deep breath, then smiled. *And so it begins!*